I0552683

Calliope 2013

The 20th Anthology of
Women Who Write

Susan E. Lindsey, Editor

Calliope 2013: the 20th Anthology of Women Who Write
Susan E. Lindsey, Editor

Published annually by
Women Who Write
P.O. Box 6167
Louisville, KY 40206-0167

Copyright © 2013 by Women Who Write, Inc. All rights reserved.
ISBN 9780988367333

This book was manufactured in the United States of America. All rights reserved. No part of this book may be reproduced in any form or by any electronic or mechanical means, including information retrieval and retrieval systems, without permission in writing from Women Who Write, Inc., except by a reviewer, who may quote brief passages in a review.

To order or for more information, see www.womenwhowrite.com. Please contact the organization at info@womenwhowrite.com for bulk orders or to schedule a reading.

Calliope

"Thou, Calliope, queen of the groves of song, uplift thy lyre and begin the tale."
—*Thebaid* 4.32

In Greek mythology, Calliope was the oldest of the nine daughters of Zeus, king of the gods, and Mnemosyne, goddess of memory. The daughters were collectively known as the nine muses; each daughter was assigned a specific literary or artistic dimension.

Calliope was the muse of epic poetry and eloquence or prose. She is often pictured holding a writing tablet and stylus, sometimes with a book or scroll, and wearing a gold crown. She inspired Homer to write the "Iliad" and the "Odyssey."

Ancient Greek writers and artists believed that any of the muses could be called upon for help, regardless of their assigned responsibility. They regularly asked their favorite muse for inspiration.

Today, a muse can be anything that inspires the flow of creative energy—meditation, music, or a special room or place. Literature abounds with artists' accounts of relationships—real and imaginary—with their muses.

The members of Women Who Write dedicate our annual anthology to women readers and writers, and to those who love them. We share the joy and productivity of those who have found their muse, and support and encourage those who still struggle in their search.

Dedicated to all women who aspire to express
themselves through the written word;
we are kindred spirits.

Contributing Member Authors

Cynthia Clegg Canada

Paula Dillmann

Joan Dubay

J. Watson Finger

Erin Fitzgerald

Margaret F. Grimes

Carroll Grossman

Holly Hinson

Charlet Johnson

Susan E. Lindsey

Maria Josefa Reyes

Kathey Schickli

Maryann Strickland

Jeannie Waldridge

Contents

About Women Who Write, Inc.

Women Who Write, Inc. is an organization of women writers who are dedicated to excellence in literary creation. Our mission is to welcome, encourage, educate, and support women who aspire to write. All women interested in writing, at any level, in any genre, amateur or professional, are invited to join.

The organization meets the first Thursday of each month at 6:30 p.m. at the Highlands-Shelby Park Branch of the Louisville Free Public Library, located at 1250 Bardstown Road in the Mid-City Mall, Louisville, Kentucky.

Annual membership dues are $50 and entitle members to participate in monthly meetings (which include readings and critiques), guest lectures, and participation in our annual retreat.

Women Who Write is a 501(c)(3) nonprofit organization. Donations are gratefully accepted to support our mission and are tax deductible.

Please visit our website, www.womenwhowrite.com, for more information.

Women Who Write Board of Directors

Susan E. Lindsey, Director

Margaret F. Grimes, Associate Director

Morgan Eklund, Secretary and Webmaster

Carroll Grossman, Treasurer

Cynthia Clegg Canada, Associate Director of Communication and Public Relations, and Newsletter Editor

About Calliope and the International Short Prose and Poetry Contest

Women Who Write is proud to present the 2013 *Calliope*, our twentieth annual anthology. The book features the work of the winners of our International Short Prose and Poetry Contest, as well as the work of our members.

The contest is open to all women writers over the age of eighteen. In 2013, we received a record 281 entries from women in thirty-three states and five countries. Winners were chosen in a blind judging by independent judges. This year, our prose judges were novelists Cynthia Ellingsen and Virginia Smith; our poetry judges were published poets Yalonda Green and Crystal Wilkinson. We extend our special thanks to them for their careful consideration of all the entries.

The winning entries in the poetry and prose categories are included in *Calliope*, in addition to works written by Women Who Write members. Our members are not eligible to win in either category, but *Calliope* offers them the opportunity to be published. For some, this is the first time their work has been published.

Please note that some of the content in this anthology may address adult themes or include language that is offensive to some people. The anthology is intended for adult readers.

This year, special thanks go to Women Who Write members Mariam Williams, *Calliope* chairperson; Morgan Eklund, who provided contest oversight; Susan Lindsey, who edited *Calliope*; and Cynthia Clegg Canada, who designed the book. Gloria (Gee) Smith designed the cover.

We want to thank the many board members and Women Who Write members who preceded us and produced *Calliope* issues one through nineteen. We hope that you enjoy these poems, stories, and essays.

Poetry Judges

Yalonda JD Green is a Cave Canem poetry fellow, vocalist, and arts educator from Detroit. She graduated from the University of Louisville with a PhD in humanities in 2011 and has whittled her creative dissertation, "That Terrifying Center: Poetry, Language, and Embodied Subjectivities," into *Fix*, her  forthcoming collection of poems. Her work has appeared in *Reverie, Mythium,* and *TORCH*. In addition to writing and performing, JD conducts singing and creativity workshops with cultural organizations throughout Metro Louisville. Her debut album, "Diurnal Movements," is an organic blend of original jazz, soul and funk. Visit music.jdgreensoul.com to listen to her music and learn about upcoming shows. Yalonda JD Green lives and jams in Louisville, Kentucky, with her husband and their three pups.

Crystal Wilkinson is the author of *Blackberries, Blackberries*, winner of the 2002 Chaffin Award for Appalachian Literature, and *Water Street*, a finalist for both the UK's Orange Prize for Fiction and the Hurston/Wright Legacy Award. Both books  are published by Toby Press. She is also the recipient of awards and fellowships from the Kentucky Foundation for Women, the Kentucky Arts Council, the Mary Anderson Center for the Arts, and the Fine Arts Work Center in Provincetown. She is the winner of the 2008 Denny Plattner Award in poetry from *Appalachian Heritage* magazine and the Sallie Bingham Award from the Kentucky Foundation for Women. She currently teaches writing and literature in the BFA in creative writing program at Morehead State University. She has also taught in the brief residency MFA in writing program at Spalding University and the MFA in creative writing at Indiana University, Bloomington. She and her partner, poet and artist Ron Davis, own the Wild Fig Bookstore in Lexington, Kentucky.

Prose Judges

Cynthia Ellingsen is the author of two contemporary women's fiction books, both published by Penguin-Berkley: *Marriage Matters* (2013) and *The Whole Package* (2011). Her novels have been translated for sale in Italy and more recently in Hungary. A former screenwriter, she co-wrote two scripts optioned by Identity Films. Currently, she teaches writing through the Carnegie Center in Lexington, Kentucky. An avid public speaker, she has been invited to speak to several professional women's organizations across the state of Kentucky.

Virginia Smith is the bestselling author of twenty-four novels, an illustrated children's book, and more than fifty articles and short stories. An avid reader with eclectic tastes in fiction, Smith writes in a variety of styles, from lighthearted relationship stories to breath-snatching suspense. Her books have been finalists for the American Christian Fiction Writers' Carol Award, the Daphne du Maurier Award of Excellence in Mystery / Suspense, the Maggie Awards, and the National Reader's Choice Awards. Two of her novels, *A Daughter's Legacy* (2011) and *Dangerous Impostor* (2013), received the Holt Medallion Award of Merit. Learn more about Virginia Smith and her books at VirginiaSmith.org.

Winners of the
2013 International
Short Prose and Poetry Contest

First Place

    Prose   *Foot Washing*, Tabatha Hibbs

    Poetry   *i miss lac du flambeau*, Selene Phillips

Second Place

    Prose   *This is a Good Idea*, Gwen Hart

    Poetry   *The Possibility of Teetering*, Harriet Shenkman

Third Place

    Prose   *Paddle Through*, Suzanne Purvis

    Poetry   *Night Probe: The Hermit Crab*, Joanne Milavec

Honorable Mention

    Prose   *The Missouri Trail*, Jan Sparkman

    Poetry   *Shelf Life*, Molly Fuller

Foot Washing

Tabatha Hibbs

Today is foot washing at church. I get up as I do each
Sunday morning, cook breakfast for Nash and the boys. Today,
it's ham and eggs. I cheat, though, and use canned biscuits. I am
too tired to mix dough, and the heft of the glass rolling pin is too
tempting: I can imagine the solid thunk it would make against
Nash's head. So I pull the paper strip from around the tin of
biscuit dough; Nash frowns at the can, but he is silent. He is not
dumb.

When we sit at the table, Nash offers grace in a voice that is
expressive only when he asks for forgiveness of sins. I think he
might be praying to me, but I am like the Old Testament God —
my heart is hard, and I will not yield to the pleadings of this
man. We fall to eating, and Caleb drags his ham through the
yolk ooze on his plate; a fat drop clings to the end of the fork. I
watch the drop as he brings the fork to his mouth and know the
yolk is going to stretch until it drips across his white shirt. I do
nothing. I am too tired to catching dripping egg yolks and too
hot in this tiny kitchen warmed from baking biscuits and the
four bodies crowded around the table. I feel the sweat pooling
beneath my sagging breasts where they hang, bra-less, under
my housedress. I think about later when the basins are brought
in, filled with cool water. There will be a sponge floating in
each — a cheap one from the Dollar Store, but it will hold water
just the same, water that will be squeezed across the bare flesh
of our feet until they are as cool as the water. I wish for that cool
water to wipe under my breast as I wipe yolk from the Formica

tabletop and Caleb's face and find another white shirt to tuck into his navy blue pants.

I dress as I do each Sunday in a clean print dress with my hair pinned up.

Except there are no stockings this week. Foot washing is the only Sunday of the year that women can go into the church without stockings. I wash up before dressing, but the heavy scent of grease and salted ham clings to me like the oily perfume Jacob gave me for Mother's Day. I hate that I always smell like the kitchen of a cheap restaurant, and I wonder if it is this scent of meals past that pushed Nash to the far side of the bed and then out the door. He does not tell me why he sinned against me, the children, and God in heaven. "I was weak" is all he tells me. Yes, weak, I think, while I am strong with grease and salt, sticky with sweat and spilled egg yolk. I take care to wash the inside of my sandals where my bare feet will rest through the service. I will carry no dirt into the church; I will not soil the basin of cool water.

When we get to church, I slide into the pew next to my mother-in-law, Corinne. Nash and Jacob move to the other side of the church. Jacob is six, old enough to sit through a service without a book or a string of beads to keep him busy, but Caleb stays with me. He is only three, too young yet to sit with the men across the aisle. Instead, he clambers onto the pew next to Corinne, then disappears into the folds of her large arms. She kisses the top of his head several times.

"It's a blessed morning," she says to me between the kisses.

"A blessed morning, indeed." I sit beside her, conscious of Nash across the aisle and two rows up. Men approach him and shake his hand. Some pat him on the back. One, Brother Raymond, lays a hand on Nash's head, lifts the other up to heaven, and prays a bit. I think again about the rolling pin and the cracking sound it might make on Nash's skull. I don't think his thick, dark curls would do much to soften the force. Then I realize that such a blow would break the rolling pin. No, that wouldn't do. It had been my grandmother's. I had watched her roll out bread and cookies, could still feel her hands over mine as I rolled out my first piecrust. I couldn't break that rolling pin . . . not on Nash.

Nash confessed his sins last week. When Brother Charles, the preacher, had stepped from behind the pulpit and raised his hands up to the heavens and asked who among them had sinned, Nash had moved from his place in the pew and gone up to the altar and told everyone how he had sinned against his family and against God. The church gradually filled with "Oh, Lord" and "yes, Lord" and "Praise God" and "Forgive him, Lord." But I had stood in a bubble of cold air, shut away from the prayers and the murmurings, had stood in this cold air that wrapped itself around me and through me. I hadn't known. I didn't feel Corinne's hug, and her "Bless you, child" reached me as through deep water. I hadn't known. There had been no missed meals or late nights working. His clothes had smelled only of his sweat, the spice of sawdust, the musk of his cattle that followed him around the pasture like giant dogs—followed him all the way to slaughter. I hadn't known. The cold radiated from me pushing out into a sphere until empty space sur-rounded me and this new knowing.

Now, I look away from Nash and feel the space about me still. Nash is the sinner, but I am the wife who couldn't keep her husband. I am the woman whose body bore two sons but was not enough to keep the man in his own bed. Women cast long glances at me, then whisper to those near them. I am pariah; I am lesson. Where had I failed? I know they ask this. I would ask this of another woman if she sat in my place. "I do not know," I want to shout across the cold that surrounds me, that is not warmed even by Corinne's large body, by the arm that squeezes my shoulder. I do not know. It is the grease. It is the heat. It is the sweat. It is all these things. It is none of these things.

I realize that I am staring at white skin. Two pews ahead of me, Grace sits as she does each week. Her two girls are on either side of her. I can see the white skin of Grace's neck in a narrow strip between the collar of her dress and the soft line of her upswept hair. The flesh is unblemished, fresh as though it has never been touched by sun or heat. It hasn't been touched much; Grace is a teller in a bank in town. I see her once a week when I take in Nash's paycheck. Sometimes I go to her window, and I envy those long, white fingers that count out the paper money so quickly. Her nails are neat, never cracked beneath the clear polish. I keep my hands folded on the counter until the last possible moment. My hands are brown, like my arms, my neck, and my face. I spend too many hours hanging clothes on the line and working the garden not to be sun-tinged. My nails are always short and chipped. I have hands of soil and detergent and a neck of sun and wind.

I envy Grace her smooth skin when I'm at the bank, and now I envy her in church. She has draped an arm around the shoulders of her older daughter and is whispering something in her ear. Grace's arm is nearly as white as the skin across her neck, but it is toned; I can see the contour of muscle. No loose skin lolls at its edges as it does on mine. I carry the last fifteen pounds of my pregnancy with Caleb in my arms and across my breasts like a wrap. I envy Grace's toned arms, her white skin, her perfect nails. I shouldn't covet, I know. It is a sin, just as Nash's adultery is a sin. Equal in God's eyes, though that seems unfair. My sin is silent and sits in a quiet corner of my heart. It does not take me away from my husband or my children. It does not worm its way into the bed of another family. I close my eyes. If I had Grace's white skin, would that have been enough?

The church is filling; it is nearly time for services to start. Soon, Delbert will go to the front of the church with his pitch pipe and call, "Ya'll gather round." Men, women, and a few children will gather round him and his rounded back will disappear behind the square shoulders of bodies much younger than his. Sheets of music will be passed around, and voices in moderate harmony will fill the area before the altar, then wash over the still seated congregation like waves breaking across shells scattered at the water's edge.

Sometimes I go to singing class and lift up my voice to the Lord. My voice is not strong, nor is it sweet, but I can carry a tune. Delbert says the Lord is more interested in the song of my heart than the song of my lips, so I let the joy or the sorrow or the gratitude of my heart wend its way into the words that swirl from my mouth. Sometimes it seems that I can nearly follow those words straight up to the Lord himself so infused are they with the song of my heart.

But I don't sing today. My heart is not the heart of a woman bowing before her Lord. It is the heart of a woman who is chilled by anger at her sinning husband, a woman who covets the skin of her neighbor. These are not the things to lift unto the Lord except in repentance. I am not repentant. I cannot lift up a sweet song of praise, and my heart is too bitter to ride on the songs of penance and sorrow. So I sit in the cold quiet corner of my heart with my envy and my wrath. I think again that I am the Old Testament God. He was jealous and vengeful. He wiped out entire peoples that did not bow before him. But my vengeance is limited. My wrath is aimed at only one. But I do not think this makes me more merciful.

No one sits in the pew with Corinne, Caleb, and me. Usually, Shelby and her daughter sit at the far end of our pew. Today, they sit two behind us, and Shelby drops her gaze when I catch her eye. I decide the space that has widened about me, space that no woman but Corinne dares to cross, is a holy space. I sit in my righteous space through the sermon and think how Nash should be punished for not holding me and my body sacred. I think of Mary Magdalene washing the feet of Christ and wish that men and women were not separated for foot washing, that Nash would bow before me and all the church and wash my feet with his tears. I hold that image for a while, caressing it, and I savor his humility and his shame before all the church.

It is when Brother Charles's fevered sermon has trickled down to a small stream and dried itself in "Yes, Lords" and "Amens" and the men begin bringing in the basins of water that I think of Jesus washing the feet of his disciples. I think of Nash's feet. They are large, the toes long, the nails rough from his tearing them rather than clipping them. There are calluses on his big toes where his steel-toed boots rub, and the arch of his left foot has flattened from the time a young bull stepped on his foot. I have rubbed his feet nearly every night before bed since we've been married, but I have not rubbed his feet this week. I have not touched him since last Sunday. For a moment, I think that I will cross to the men's side of the church, kneel before my husband, and wash his feet, heap my wrath upon his head in coals of kindness. But no. I like the stillness of my heart. I like the cold space around me. It is quiet in the chill, and I do not want it warmed by his heat. I give up the image of his flattened foot and his callused toes, and move into the altar area with the other women.

I have just dried Corinne's feet when I feel a light touch on my shoulder, so light it seems just the brush of a skirt hem. I don't turn at first. Tears are streaming down my face, and I am tight in the chest. I am grateful to wash Corinne's feet, to show her that I love her even though her son has sinned against me. To hold another's feet in your hands, to wash them is to show more love than I want to most days. You learn a person when you hold her feet, smoothing the cool water across the skin. Corinne has a large callus on her right big toe; she tends to stand with most of her weight on that foot because her left knee hurts so much. The skin across the top of her feet is parchment thin and crisp, crossed-hatched with blue veins so thin they seem painted on. I wonder how she ignores the corn crusting across the top of her second toe, how long the sore has been festering on the side of her heel. I realize that Corinne is not a young woman. Her diabetes ages her, and I know that there cannot be many years more before her body gives up to the sugar and to the weight.

The touch brushes my shoulder again. I turn, and Grace is standing above me with a basin balanced on her hip. The fingertips of her right hand linger on my shoulder. The perfect white skin of her face is blotched red from sobbing. Her eyes look bruised as though she has not slept. I wonder if she's been sick, remember that she wasn't at her bank window on Friday.

"I'd like to wash your feet." Her voice is a whisper, hard to hear amidst the wails of the women about me and the sobs the men cough into their chests where they kneel on the far side of the church.

My hand goes to my chest. "Me?" I have no idea why this woman I barely know wants to wash my feet. Foot washings are between people who are close—friends and family. I have never washed the feet of anyone other than Corinne and Rachel, my closest church friend. No one but Rachel has ever held in her hands the map of my daily walk.

Grace holds her hand out to balance me as I stand and turn to seat myself on the bench next to Corinne. Corinne pulls me close, whispers her love into my ear, then rises with her basin to rinse out and refill. I know that she will find Rose, her closest friend, and the two will wash each other's aging feet as they do each year.

I slip my feet from my shoes, suddenly aware of how stubby my toes seem compared to the length of my foot, very aware of the little toe that had been mangled by a misdirected garden hoe years before. I pull my feet back under the pew and begin reaching for my shoes. Grace's hand brushes against my wrist, again so lightly as to seem little more than a breath of air. She shakes her head, and my hand falls slack beneath her touch. Her hand moves to my right foot, lifts it into the basin. Pushing the sponge aside, Grace cups her hands and lifts the water toward my ankle. When the tepid liquid splashes across my skin, a shiver settles across my shoulders, a shiver like those elicited by Nash's breath on my neck when he still pulled me close in the dark of our bed.

Her left hand cups my foot, her right hand scooping water across the skin, fingertips slipping across the terrain of my foot as though she could read my past in my mangled toe, my present in the hard ridge of my heel. Grace is not crying although her chest moves with the deep heaves of sobs. My own tears have dried, and I close my eyes as she wraps my foot in the Dollar Store towel. I feel the heat of her hand through the thin fabric. I lean into this touch. Not my body—it stays rigid on the bench, separate from this me who wants the smooth white hand with the perfect nails to slide from my foot up my ankle, then to my calf, to hold my leg with the same firm pressure. It has been seven days since I have touched Nash or allowed him to touch me. Not even a brush of a kiss across the cheek before he leaves for work. I am as a land parched from no rain. I soak up Grace's touch, feel it soak through the towel, through my skin, easing the arid edges of my being.

I watch the top of Grace's head while she washes my left foot. The part of her dark hair marks the center of her head—

white scalp peeks through impossibly black hair. I want to trace my finger along the part the way her fingers are tracing the lines of my foot. When her hands slip to the cave of my foot's arch, Grace looks at me. My breath catches, and my soul falls into the palm of her hand. For a moment, she holds my very being. There have been times in the dark of our room, in the warmth of our quilts when Nash and I have made love that I felt he held my soul. There have been times at the altar when the prayers have risen about me like the voices of God's own angels that I have felt my soul leap forth to meet the Holy Spirit, and I have known for that moment that God held my soul. But I have always wrestled for my soul. It has always been mine to keep. Now though, when Grace looks at me and my soul falls into the palm of her hand, I let it go. I think she might wash it away in the basin or clutch it forever in her hand so that I will be empty always of desire, of free will. That my days will be spent in an endless repetition of cooking, cleaning, caring for my children with no awareness of a moment other than the one I am now in. I stare back hard at Grace.

Keep my soul. Hold it in your hands. Wring my soul out in the sponge until it spews out with the water into the basin. Leave me empty. I can live if I am empty.

But Grace returns my soul in a firm stroke across the cave of my instep, and I feel my being working its way into the corners of my body, settling into myself. I am aware again of the wails about me, the weeping of the women both seated and on the floor, of the choked sobs of the men across the church where they wash the feet of those they hold in highest esteem or of those who hold their greatest debts.

Then my foot is dried and returned to the floor beside the other; Grace stands and lifts the basin in a fluid moment, smooth as water itself moving across a slope. I stand, touch her arm. I want to wash her feet, to cup her heel in my hand, to hold for just a moment that which makes her Grace. But the service is nearly over. The preacher is calling for prayer. The basin disappears, then Grace is gone, lost in the shuffle of women moving toward the altar to kneel in prayer.

I stand, still feel her hand in the cave of my foot, my spirit cave. I want to tuck away this echo of her touch, to put it up like the vegetables of my garden, stores against the winter. But the touch memory is fading already, even as I kneel among the women crowding at the altar, even as I feel my soul settling back into the corners of my body. It leaves an emptiness, a space within that was Grace and her touch. *This* is my store against the winter that is, that will come.

i miss lac du flambeau

Selene Phillips

Every morning I wake up, and I look out the window.
Some people think I live in a city. So one might think I see the
　　　other building across the street.
But i don't.
One would think I see the paved streets and the organized
　　　sidewalks.
But i don't.
You might believe I see the new buildings under construction.
But i don't.
Instead, i see what i really want to see. Instead, i see home.
Instead, i see water . . .
　　　　lots and lots of water . . .

~ ~ ~ ~ ~ ~ ~ ~ ~ ~ lakes ~ ~ ~ ~ ~ ~ ~ ~ ~ ~ ~

~　~　~　~　~　~　~　~　~　rivers　~　~　~　~　~　~　~　~　~

~　　~　　~　　~　　& streams　　~　　~　　~　　~

i see trees . . . a forest of green

^^^^^^^^^^^ evergreen ^^^^^^^^^^^

^ ^ ^ ^ ^ ^　white pine　^ ^ ^ ^ ^ ^

V v V V v V v birch V v V V v V v

i see the green pine trees and the water.

i see a sun so bold it doubles itself on the shimmering waters, our famous chain of lakes.

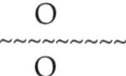

flaming waters . . . flaming torches . . . lake of the torches . . .

♀ ♀ ♀ ♀ ♀ ♀ ♀

I miss how one state can have such a varied landscape.
The plains-like center and dairy farms
The potato fields in the upper middle
The cliffs of the west
The lake to the east
My Milwaukee uncles and cousins would tease me as they gave
    directions to navigate in the big city . . .
        If you're in the water, you've gone too far!
Another sacred beautiful lake at the top . . .
        The top border of Michigan's Upper Peninsula
And alas . . . ahhhh . . . up north . . . UP NORTH!

I miss hearing the words "up north." We all knew what "up north" meant. For all of you southerners who occupy the earth anywhere below the Lake Tomahawk and Wausau area. Up north means woods. It means water. More woods. It means family. Woods. It means home.
The woods. I'm going in the woods. I'm going to the woods. I work in the woods. I'll be in the woods.

i am in the woods.
    i live in the woods.
        i live in the woods.
            i live in the woods.
As i sit here surrounded by the physical and metaphysical
hierarchy of "ivory towers" and cement, buildings that mark
this metropolis horizon, I think of the woods. And i can smell air
that combines pine trees, sandy soil, inland fresh waters and
overactive photosynthesis operating in surround-sound.
I miss seeing brown faces with black or dark brown hair. Men
wearing red-and-black plaid woolen shirts, the kind they wore
to go into the woods. The kind of shirts for lumber work and for
hunting, before blaze orange kept everyone safer from the city
crazies.
And as much as I hate to see a tree chopped down, i even miss
seeing lumber,
                lumberyards
          timber trucks
      lumbermen
    & lumberwomen.

i miss hearing hunting stories. i'm going hunting. i got a buck. i
got a doe. i got a ten-pointer. i miss hearing about how my
cousin Monica was a better huntress than most men.
I also miss seeing women wearing aprons. i miss venison
             wild rice
                walleye
                     muskie
                        perch
i miss gathering and or hunting it and eating it.

In this land of Southern belles and racehorses, i miss snow. i
miss winter. biboon, biboonagad

Snow . . .

    snow . . .

        snow . . .

            snow . . .

                and . . .

                    more snow . . .

i miss snow. Real snow. i miss the kind of snow where snowing is the weather's business.

And the different names of snow. The ojibwemowin snow.
Onaabanad—crust on the snow
    ishpaagonagaa—deep snow
        zhakipon—heavy wet falling snow
            goonikaa—lots of snow
                bimipon—snow going along
                    mamaangadepon—large flakes of snow
                        zhakaagonagaa—soft snow
                          maajipon—starting to snow
                            anaamaagon—under the snow
Flakes,
Huge manna of chunky flakes
Stuck-together flakes
Lots of tiny drops
Many tiny circles or pellets
Lots of different sizes, shapes, surfaces, skeletons, symmetries, spirits
With their different sensations, senses, shadows, surprises, sensitivity, and sympathy
If you listen, sensational snowflakes tell secrets of scandal and slander.
But most teach sensibility.

i miss me being part of the snow
    falling in the snow
        slipping on the snow
            sliding on the snow
                skating over the snow
                    swallowing snow
                        wallowing in the snow
                          melting snow

being cold in the snow
    being snowbound
        being sad in the snow
            being silent in the snow
                being content in the snow
                  being consigned to the snow

i miss all kinds of snow
                              heavy snow
                          soft snow
                      mild snow
                  falling snow
                drifting snow
              hard snow
            blinding snow
        snowed under
      frosty snow
    slushy snow
  snowy nights
whiteouts

snow
*   snow
 *   *   snow
  *   snow
*   *   snow

```
     *        *              snow
   *      *         *      *  snow
   *              *               snow
      *          * *      *       snow
         *                 *          snow
     *            *   *      *     snow
  *          *   *          *        *      *   *   *snow
                             *               snow
     *     *           *      *   *              *        snow
         *                *         * *       *        snow
   *
           *      *
 snow                        *
 *         *          *         snow *
   *   *     snow       *     *     *      *
     *              *       *     *        *      snow
 *             *          snow  *         *
       *  snow    *         *          *          *    *
     *      *    snow         *    snow      *          *
 *             *      *              *      snow  *
       *    *      snow        *      snow
 snow     *     *               *        *  snow      *
 *     *            *        *     snow                *
     *     snow              *      *      *              *
 *            *      *           *            snow    *
     *      *            *       *    snow        *
       *          *snow        *                 *
     *       *
```

a blessing of snow . . .

snow to play in
      snow to shovel
            snow to drive in
                  snow to remove
                        snow to build snowmen with

                snow to throw
            snow to build forts with
                snow to melt
                snow to eat
                snow to drink
              snow to dance with
                snow to pee in
                 snow for you
                 snow for me
                 snow to love
From roofs, ^
    From front doors []
        From cars o # o
          From driveways, ll
             From trails - - -
               From roads ===
                 From seemingly everywhere

i miss seeing snowshoes, aagimose.
mikwam
daashkikwadin
babaamaadagaako
animaadagaako
niminaaweyaadagaako
inaadagaako
bimaadagaako
i miss ice fishing, akwa'waa

i miss ice-skating, zhooshokwaada'aagan.

i miss being bound by the weather. i miss its interruption of our
schedule. The way it commands us to pay attention. The way it
seeks to constantly outdo itself with record chills below zero
and record snowfalls. The way it alters our plans.

In the city, people pretend to own the weather. They refuse to let it dictate their lives.

They melt it, shovel it, remove it, curse it, plow it.

But they never make peace with it.

They are ungrateful with their requests for warmer, colder, less humidity and more sunshine.

Before the late 80s and early 90s, i miss how people would react when we said we were from Lac du Flambeau. Most would defiantly reply, "I've lived in Wisconsin all my life. I've never heard of *that* town before," as if we didn't exist. We were from a place outside of *their* Wisconsin.

Now too many seemingly and smugly and knowingly smile, like they know a secret. They've already judged us. They appreciate the beauty of our lakes and trees, but the "Ojibwe take all the fish . . ."

i miss a place where the white northern pine's branches look like God's arms.

Where David and i climbed nearly to the top of a white pine one day, fifty feet into the clean clear summertime air. Aunt Alice looked for us and yelled, but we were carefully hidden among the evergreens, giggling. I was so brave following him up. Once in the clouds, I wondered how I would ever get down. The reverse direction was not so easy. He had to climb down first. Again I had to follow.

i miss the bar runs. A dozen of us kids would pile into a rundown station wagon and Uncle Pete would direct a few of his nieces, our mothers, to an out-of-the-way bar. Out-of-the-way meant that the drive would take at least an hour via an abandoned old lumber road. It also meant we would be gone all day. We were guaranteed treats of plastic jars of bubbles, Dutch potato chips, sodas, and bags of pre-popped popcorn. Being left in the car alone to rule ourselves. We'd have to stop and pee at the side of the road. There were no roadside rest areas.

i miss Mabel's old house nestled among the pine and the old horseshoe dirt road leading to it.

i even miss the outhouse, a double-seater. i miss the barn-like structure in back. The rusty rundown pieces of equipment i could not recognize. i miss seeing where i imagined Spot and Sandy were hitched for a sleigh ride to fetch a Christmas tree.

i miss the huge old lilac bush out back. Millions of lilac petals would produce the sweetest smelling backyard. It was the girls' playhouse if we got there first and the boys' outhouse if they beat us to it.

i miss the old rusty basketball rim and the glorious sound of kerdunk . . . splat splat . . . kerdunk . . . splat splat . . . as a couple of young boys would help themselves to a pick-up game and the ball would drop in a puddle of water.

i miss seeing the Stone's tiny square home that housed thirteen kids and the dirt and mud that would separate us.

i miss the homely green or bright ugly blue government housing paint.

i miss hearing miigwetch and boozhoo, grandma's ever-welcoming "biindige, biindige," asking anyone whose shadow hit her door to come in.

i miss walking up town. i miss swimming off State Road 70.

i miss dragonflies hatching. i miss Sand Beach.

i miss the sign that said "Unincorporated."

God i miss Lac du Flambeau.

Mostly i miss the stories. The old ones. The new ones that are created every day. The ones that will never be written down. The ones that will eventually be forgotten. The ones that will manifest themselves into lore and take on new meaning.

Does colonization ever really stop? Does the movement ever really die?
Or is it just transformed into something less familiar, like an institute for higher education?

I may work and own a home in Louisville. People think I'm a professor here. They see my body come and go. I read, write, teach. I have lunch. I converse. I make conversation. I like my colleagues. I like my office with a new window that overlooks the downtown Louisville skyline. But i'm not really here. I don't really occupy space in this big city. My body may cross the Wisconsin-Illinois; Illinois-Indiana; Indiana-Kentucky border, but i still LIVE in Lac du Flambeau. i'm there every day. i float above the waters and glide among the trees. There, i am me. My dreams come alive and hope wells there.
My heart stays there where it is safe.

Gitchie-manito . . .
   great mystery
     Creator . . .
       i miss lac du flambeau.

Make sure my body ends up there
   across from Sand Beach
     in the cemetery with Harvey and Mabel
   Uncle Pete
     Aunt Ginger
       Uncle Tom
        Aunt Alma and Uncle Jack
         other cousins
          & friends

And others who were killed by the heartache of colonization,
        genocide, and stolen land.

Make sure someone makes me an Ojibwe house out of old
wooden boards.
Make sure someone says a prayer in Ojibwemowin.
Make sure i get home
Send me home please
miigwetch

This Is a Good Idea

Gwen Hart

Sam is tall and lanky, with a pointed chin, round silver-rimmed glasses, and curly white-blonde hair. The skin on the back of his hands is translucent, almost as if he has rubbed it down to a smooth, thin layer of cellophane. In the adult ed. fiction writing class he teaches, he sits hunched over as if he has a stomachache and speaks very quietly, so quietly I have to lean forward to hear him across the conference table. I feel an instinctual need to protect him.

On the first day, he whispers that he is allergic to most scented products, including cigarettes, perfume, hairspray, lotions, and deodorant. He cannot abide even the residual scent leftover from most soaps and shampoos. If we want to stay in the class, we have to wash our hair with fragrance-free baby shampoo beforehand and clean our clothes using unscented detergent.

My best friend Wendy kicks me under the table. I kick her back, harder. Wendy did not want to take this class; she wanted to take Italian cooking. I reminded her that she was on a diet, and convinced her fiction writing would be a better idea. Now Wendy tilts up her notebook at me. On it she has written, "This is not a good idea" in gothic letters. She pops a gum bubble.

Sam winces. "Please," he whispers, "no gum." He covers his nose and mouth with his pale hand and turns as white as the paper in front of him. "Watermelon," he mouths, his eyes tearing up.

Wendy squints at me, tears the page out of her notebook, wads the gum up in it and throws it away.

While Sam is passionately explaining the importance of first sentences to us, his bony right elbow comes perilously close to knocking over his hot water with honey. I am seized by a vivid image of the steaming water sloshing over, burning holes in his pale, sensitive skin. If this happens, I feel I could not bear it. It would be as if I myself were being burned. At the next class, I sit in the chair to his right, hovering close in case of disaster. Once, I move the glass mug just in time. That's when he first notices I exist, fixing me with his eyes. They are the color of faded denim, as light as the jeans Wendy and I bleached one summer and then washed and washed until most of the color leached away.

At the Wicked Chicken Bar after class, Wendy rolls her eyes and complains about Sam's soft voice, the way he wrings his hands, and his critique of her character study of a prostitute with mismatched fishnet stockings who tries to save a drowning deer and gets kicked into a coma in the process.

"Sam is a published novelist and a reclusive genius," I remind her. "It takes all his energy to come to class. You should be thanking him for telling you your story is crap."

"Have you got a crush on him?" asks Wendy. "That is not a good idea. Do you really want to get involved with someone you can't wear hairspray around?" Hairspray is very important to Wendy. She drops out of fiction writing, but I hang in there, sitting right next to Sam week after week. I receive an A-.

After the last class, Sam asks me if I will stay for a few minutes. He says it so quietly I'm not sure I've heard him correctly, but I take my time putting my notebook and pencil in my bag, just in case.

Sam and I are married at the courthouse by a justice of the peace. I carry a bouquet of silk flowers so Sam won't be sneezing and red-eyed in the photos. (He still has to sit down with his head between his knees when Wendy accidentally uses the flash.) Wendy serves as photographer and witness, even though she reminds me in the courthouse bathroom before the ceremony that she does not think this is a very good idea.

"Wendy," I say, hissing at the stall door dividing us, "stop saying that."

Wendy twists up her mouth when I tell her about the duplex Sam asked me to pick out so that we can live together, but apart.

Sam's writing desk is on the other side of the wall from where I sit on my living room couch. Coco, my Newfoundland dog, is slobbering on a bone at my feet. If I concentrate, I can picture Sam on the other side of the wall, with his green-hooded desk lamp and his clean white desk. There's not one crumb, not one water-ring on that desk. Or anywhere else in Sam's half of the duplex. When he is thinking through ideas, Sam cleans with a damp cloth and a mask over his nose and goggles over his eyes to protect him from particles of lead, arsenic, and DDT lurking in the dust. Sam writes each sentence painstakingly. He wrings his hands and worries through each word, each phrase. Once he has a sentence down, he never goes back and fiddles with it. His sentences are always perfect.

Sam cannot be bothered when he is writing. He must have clean, uninterrupted time and space to think up those perfect sentences. I respect his creative process and tiptoe around my half of the duplex as much as possible. When I listen to AC/DC, I put my headphones on and do not sing along.

When we bought the duplex, Sam made it sound romantic. I suppose to a reclusive genius just knowing someone is on the other side of the wall breathing is romantic enough.

I should be fair. There is the door. Sam had it installed the first week we moved in, an interior door that allows access between the two halves of the duplex. Sam kept insisting that the carpenter leave a gap measuring exactly one inch under the bottom of the door. I didn't understand why he was so concerned about the gap under the door, but it didn't matter. I was so happy, imagining how I would pop in on him throughout the day, bringing him a cup of hot water with honey, asking him how his writing was going. He would read me a scene and I would clap my hands in delight or rub his shoulders encouragingly, working out the knots. He would ask me what I was making for dinner, and I would tell him about the lovely piece of salmon I found at the grocery. I would regale him with the ingredients of the mustard sauce. Later that evening, we would eat dinner in my half of the duplex, by candlelight.

Most of the time, Sam keeps the door between the two halves of the duplex closed and locked. He has the only key. When he finishes a chapter, he prints it out and slides it under the door for me to read. That is why he was so concerned about the one-inch gap.

We do not eat on my side of the duplex because Sam cannot abide the smell of bread toasting or steam evaporating from a pot of soup; it makes him ill. He can eat a chicken and couscous salad, for example, but it has to be served cold, with no sauce. I cook the chicken early in the day and put it in the refrigerator to chill. The scent of a lit candle, even plain beeswax, makes Sam's eyes water. I have tried electric candles, but they just aren't the same, and they still emit positive ions that make Sam's eye twitch.

Sometimes, despite all of my careful preparations, Sam can't eat the dinner I've brought over, and he has to go lie down with a cool washcloth on his forehead. He is so thin I have to use a shish-kabob skewer to poke another hole in his belt. I worry about him. I beg him to eat and he manages just two water crackers, half a slice of cheese.

We don't fight very often. It is difficult to argue with a reclusive genius. One thing we disagree on is children. I do not think we will ever have any children. It is difficult to have

children when you live on separate sides of a duplex. It is difficult to have children when there is a wall between you.

Once, we had a big fight about the locked door and the gap
underneath it and the lack of children. "Are you going to stick
your dick under there?" I yelled through the door. "Will it fit
under there, through the one-inch gap?" I banged on the door
with the palm of my hand. "Then maybe we'd have some kids,"
I said. Sam just turned out the light on his side of the duplex. I
could see it go out in the gap under the door.

Then I remembered the noise-canceling headphones I had
bought him for his birthday. He said he needed them so that he
could concentrate on his writing. He said that he could hear
Coco's toenails when she walked across the floor; he said he
could hear her jowls slap together when she drank water.

Sam can be passionate. Once in a while, in the middle of the
night, the phone will ring. Sam has a system with the phone.
One rings means he needs more blank paper. Two rings mean
he needs something to eat. I can take a cold plate of chicken, seal
it a plastic bag and slide it under the door. Three rings mean I
can pick up the phone.

Sometimes, in the middle of the night, when the phone rings
three times and I answer it, Sam asks me to come over. I turn the
doorknob and feel a delicious thrill run down my spine as the
door opens effortlessly under my hand. I walk up the stairs and
slip into bed next to him. As I said, he is passionate; his touch
feels as light as silk scarves brushing my breasts, my thighs.
When I wake up a few hours later, though, he is gone, at his
desk, writing a sex scene, no doubt. This is being a muse in the
strictest sense. It is not as flattering as you would think.

It's two o'clock in the afternoon when the phone rings, not
one ring, not two rings, but three whole rings.

It must be Wendy.

But it's not Wendy—it's Sam! For a moment, I am overjoyed. He has called; he has called to speak to me. But there is something strange. I hear the television in the background. There is no television in Sam's half of the duplex. When he is in the same room with an operating television, the electromagnetic radiation makes him light-headed.

"Sam," I say into the receiver, "what is that noise?"

His voice has a quality, an excited edge I have only heard when he's talking about the rising action of a story. He is not calling from the other side of the duplex, he explains. He is calling from *inside the book*. His voice is high-pitched and louder than usual.

"Where are you?" I ask.

"I'm inside the story," he says again. "I've immersed myself. Completely."

"What are you talking about?" I say. My heart is beating a little faster. "Is this some kind of thought exercise? Are you listening to NPR?"

"I've entered the novel," says Sam. "I've broken the fourth wall. Entered whole cloth. It's amazing!"

"Sam," I say, rushing over to the door. "Why don't you unlock the door, and I'll come over and you can explain it to me?"

I press my left ear against the door; I can hear him on the phone in my right ear, with the white noise in the background, but I can't hear him on the other side of the door. Could he be upstairs? I jiggle the doorknob. Locked.

"Oh, I don't know how it will end!" he exclaims. "I'm sorry, but I have to go. They have the most intricate pastries here. The crust looks like apricot lace. And the texture of the wallpaper is like the skin of a ripe avocado." There is a clatter as he puts down the phone without hanging it up.

"Sam!" I yell, "This is not a good idea!"

But he is no longer listening to me. He is having a conversation with some of his characters. They are in a café. I hold my breath and hear the silverware clinking and two women laughing. They are so happy that their writer, a reclusive genius, has decided to join them.

I want to call Wendy but I don't dare hang up the phone. I am desperate—how can I get the door open? Then I have a vivid flashback—I am standing in the hallway of Chickory High School, serving as the lookout while Wendy picks the lock to the gym teacher's office. Thank God for Wendy and her stupid crushes and her goddamned hairpins! I put the phone on speaker and dump out the mug of pencils on my desk until I find what I am looking for—two jumbo paperclips I can straighten into lock picks. I take a deep breath, fiddle with the lock, and it clicks open.

Sam's computer is on. His chair is empty.

Words are appearing on the screen. Not at Sam's usual, slow, methodical pace, but rapidly, feverishly, at the pace of real life. It is a living story.

My heart is racing. I squat down and read what is taking shape on the screen. I can barely keep up. Sam's adventures are unfolding in first person. Sam is happy; that much is clear. He is surrounded by his characters. There are sights and sounds and smells, but never more than he can handle, and since it is all in his imagination, it is not threatening at all, even to a reclusive genius. He writes that he is able to feel for the first time. That he is taking deep breaths into his lungs. He orders escargot with butter and garlic from the menu. I can't believe it. In real life, just a discussion about eating snails would be enough to make Sam take to his bed for days at a time.

"Sam," I say, pleading with the screen, "Sam, please, this is not a good idea."

What can I do? I try the keyboard, tentatively at first, just the letter "I" to begin with, then more, but it's no use. I am locked out.

Slowly, I sink down on the couch, setting the laptop down on the desk with a clunk. I am too stunned to cry. Sam's story rolls on without me. This is not the way it was supposed to be. There were supposed to be shoulder rubs and candlelit dinners. The door was supposed to be open.

I see the word *seaside* flash by out of the corner of my eye and bury my face in my hands. Sam and I did not honeymoon at the ocean because Sam said inhaling saltwater would make his eyes swell shut, and the foam would turn his toes scaly and purple.

Something moves in the doorframe dividing the duplex, and I shrink back in fear. It is Coco standing tentatively in the doorway, her massive frame hesitating, one bear paw quivering above the wood floor. She has never been in this side of the duplex before. She has put her nose through only because she has heard me banging on the keyboard. She is concerned.

"It's okay, Co," I say, and she gives a half-wag of her tail and lumbers into the room, swinging her great head from side to side and sniffing the air. It smells like . . . like nothing in here, since no food has ever been cooked on this side of the dividing wall, no perfume has ever been sprayed. Coco looks up at me, and I pat the couch cushion. She steps up, turns herself around, and curls up next to me. I rub her warm side as Sam's story continues to unfold across the computer screen. Then I begin to laugh. The sheer absurdity catches me—Coco on Sam's spotless couch; Sam living in an unfinished novel—and I laugh again.

I stroke Coco and thoughts begin to poke through like starlight into the dark recesses of my brain: 1. My name is on the bills, the bank accounts, and the duplex title (reclusive geniuses cannot be bothered with such things). 2. I can do anything I want to and no one is going to be disturbed.

I pull myself up off the couch and walk over to the alphabetized books on Sam's bookcase. I start with Edward Abbey, *Desert Solitaire*, and knock the book off the shelf. Coco jerks her head up, ears puffed out in alarm.

"It's okay, Co," I say. I knock more books down—a C, a D, and an F. They fall with great smacks, like birds grown too heavy to fly. They lay splayed open, some of their spines snapped. I do not pick them up. They are beautiful and broken. I pull a chair out from the table and knock it on its side. I rough up the rug with my foot.

Instead of seeing only one side of the duplex, I am starting to see the whole picture. I will knock down the wall just as I knocked down the books. I will adopt more dogs and let them sleep wherever they want, all over the furniture. I will live my life in messy, unfinished drafts, open and public. It may or may not be genius, but it will be mine. I can't wait to call Wendy. I know exactly what she will say.

The Possibility of Teetering

Harriet L. Shenkman

Aphrodite wore elevator shoes,
Venetian courtesans chopines.
Defiant in stilettos, daughter, you

outfox opponents in court, turn heads
on the dance floor. My mother begged
me not to move out of our iron-fenced

building, but I carted my record albums, a
worn copy of Lady Chatterley, to a flat
across the East River. My mother climbed

the stairs, handed me a dense package, two
pounds of chuck meat, ground twice. Rode
the subway back to Brooklyn, sure my

doormat strewn with daises would attract
men up to no good. You, daughter, will
move in above a disco bar, throw a

welcome party, your stilettos clicking on
a mat festooned with hearts. I'll question
the stilettos, the lure of toe cleavage,

the possibility of your teetering.
But no, I will not. I will not
climb the stairs bearing meat.

Paddle Through

Suzanne Purvis

Afraid? Of the Dark? Me?

Never.

Until now.

Having visions of your dead dad changes a guy's view of the Dark.

For fifteen years, I've never needed a night light, hall light, or bathroom light left on. But tonight I clutch my granddad's tarnished flashlight under my right arm like it's a football, and I just caught the Hail Mary pass. Not that I've ever played high school football.

I creep across the sagging linoleum of my granddad's cabin and inch open the squeaking, creaking screen door. Because despite being ancient-old, my granddad's not hard of hearing. The door's hinges squeal, sounding like screams that could wake the dead. Crap. I hope not.

I open the wooden screen enough to squeeze through. Then close it, with more squeals from the hinges. Outside, I listen. Silence. I made it. Into the Dark.

The cabin sits in the middle of a bunch of trees, mostly cedar and spruce, which makes the Dark smell like Christmas, which should be comforting. It's not. Dead Dad hated Christmas. A memory detonates and I hear his voice. "Too much commercialism for such a holy holiday."

I hum a raunchy rap song to squash the memory, something my therapist suggested. My eyes adjust, my heartbeat slows, and individual tree trunks emerge from the Dark. To the right, the path to the lake. I suck it up and step down onto the first stair.

Thud. Creak. Groan.

Stupid loudmouth steps. Forget this. I launch myself.

Snap. Snap. Pop.

Sounds like gunshots as I land on loose twigs.

Crouched on the damp dirt, I hold my breath and look back at the cabin—no movement, no lights, no sound. I exhale and switch on the flashlight. The beam flickers and fades. I shake it. Another flicker and then a weak glimmer barely makes it to the mossy ground in front of me. Stupid hunk of metal. I shake it again and the glimmer grows stronger.

I skulk along the timeworn path. Bats scoot and skim among the overhead branches, whooshing, and close enough to ruffle my hair. I involuntarily duck and flinch. "Bats eat the mosquitoes. Good guys to have around," my granddad likes to say. I don't think so. Not in the Dark. I speed up.

The trees end near the shore and a half moon hangs over the dead calm lake. Not so dark here. I shut off the useless flashlight. The reflected moon colors the water a shimmering slate, but everything else appears as black silhouettes. The opposite shoreline, the dock, the boathouse, all etched as if by a heavy black marker. The dead tree branch jutting over the water, benign during the day, now looks like a fat, spidery crack on a windshield, threatening to shatter the lake.

I turn on the sickly flashlight.

"Never much use that one."

My heart slams in my chest. The flashlight falls and clatters against a rock. My granddad chuckles.

"Might not be any use now." He pushes himself out of a webbed and rusted lawn chair. His knees crack and pop more than my breakfast cereal.

"What the hell, Granddad. You scared the crap out of me. I thought you were sleeping."

"Yeah, I guessed that by the way you jumped." He shuffles over to me, his World's Best Granddad mug glued to his crooked fingers. He insists I gave him the mug. Maybe. When I was like two. I wish he'd stop using it.

He takes a slow sip, sounding like a deflating whoopee cushion. "I know why I'm up. Old. Can't sleep more than a few hours at a time. What's your excuse? I thought teenagers slept like the dead."

That word again. "Yeah well, who can sleep when it's so quiet?" Just then a loon cries from somewhere in this watery, rural hellhole. A splash follows, as a fish leaps.

Even in the dark, I can see my granddad grin. "Not so quiet. But not what you're used to in the city."

"Sure." I shift away from him, not wanting to get a whiff of what's in his mug.

He turns to look across the lake. "There's enough moonlight. You could take out John Boy. Check out the island."

How did he know?

He makes a show of taking a long deep breath through his nose. "Yup. I can smell them."

"Sure. Whatever. I guess I'll check it out." I stalk over to the wooden kayak my granddad calls John Boy. Most of my granddad's glory day stories circle back to this boat he built "when he was about my age." This morning, he hooked me into needing to paddle this rotting termite trap across the lake.

The bait he'd hooked me with wasn't the boat, but the smell. A stench that floats over the lake. I'm used to it now, and I figured it was overflowing septic tanks. But according to my granddad, it's festering snakes. On Snake Island. Too many snakes and not enough food, so his story goes. The wriggly things die and rot, belly up, on the island's pebbled beach about a mile across the lake from our shore.

Of course, I hadn't wanted him to know I was going on his "Snake Island Adventure." Wasn't much else to do in this horse-and-buggy land. I'd read all the graphic novels I'd brought. Why not check out decomposing snakes? So I'd snuck out, into the Dark, defying the living and the dead.

"Nice night to paddle." Granddad leans over John Boy, and with a boney hand pulls out the hand-carved oar. It drips.

I peer down at an inch of water in the bottom of the kayak. "Where'd the water come from? It didn't rain."

"The bow's sitting in the lake. John Boy might have a small leak or two."

"Of course it does," I muttered. My granddad had yapped on about using plywood, old nails, and leftover blue marine paint to build the thing.

He reaches into the boat and comes up with a rusty, empty soup can. "That's what this is for. Your bailing bucket." He laughs and slaps my back—hard. His calluses catch on my hoodie. He must sense the absurdity of paddling a leaking boat a mile across the lake because he straightens and grunts. "I likely have some marine putty in the shed. We could patch the seams. If you're worried . . . about a little water."

Sounds like he's calling me chicken. I grab the can and shove the stern off the sand. "I'm not worried."

He hands me the paddle. "Might want to take off your shoes." Then he sips from that stupid mug and offers it to me. "Here. Fuel for your trip."

I try not to breathe. The aroma burns my nostrils. It lingers. Fills my lungs. Invades my chest. Creeps toward my heart. And I know what's next. Dead Dad.

My granddad waves the mug around. "Strong enough to put hair on your chest. Not like those girly drinks. A latte? What the hell is that? " Then he holds his man-coffee right under my nose.

Dead Dad memories spread faster than a viral video. My dad's baritone echoes over the lake. "Let's go, Dan. Waffle World awaits. Where the coffee is black and the waitresses are stacked."

I hurl myself into the boat to escape. The force shifts John Boy free from the shallow water. Squatting in my soaked shoes, I ram the paddle into the lake, hit the sand bottom, and shove.

"Wait," my granddad calls.

I don't.

I alternate sides dipping and pulling, like I'm paddling through wet concrete. It works. We make our getaway, John Boy and I.

Whiz. Smack.

The flashlight crash-lands in the pointed bow.

"You'll need this," my granddad calls.

"Jeez. You could've hit me."

"Not a chance. I was a pitcher in high school. Land John Boy west of the big pine. More snakes there. Or so your dad said . . ."

My dad's voice rolls in over my granddad's fading words. "Need a lift, Dan?"

Splash. The sound of my paddling cuts into the memory. My dad's last words. "I can drop you off." Splash. "I'm on my way to the pool." Splash.

That stupid university pool. Three times a week he swam laps. I'd never begrudged his swim—until his last day.

"Going to hit twenty-one miles. Same as swimming the English Channel," he'd said on that day. But he'd said it a lot of other days, too. Ever since he saw the movie of the scrawny old English dude who decided to swim the Strait of Dover. Ever since the movie, my dad counted his laps as if he were making that swim. Every week he'd crossed the channel. Except—

Splash. His last week.

I paddle faster and harder.

The haunting question invades. Why didn't I take his ride? We might have come to Kirkwood and Walnut Street five minutes later. Instead, I grunted it was too early for me. He laughed and said maybe some caffeine would help. Then he offered me his travel mug. The stainless steel one I keep in my knapsack, back in the cabin, under the bed. I'd taken the sip— my first and last sip of coffee. I should've drank slower. I should've savored the whole cup. I should've gone with him.

The taste of the bitter brew seeps into my mouth. I suck up saliva and spit into the lake.

Clouds roll over the moon. The lake darkens. The Dark deepens.

I shiver and look down. Three inches of cold water cover the bottom of the boat. Crap. Using the rusted soup can, I fill and slosh water over the side. Over and over. Fill and slosh. I fixate on the shrinking level of liquid in the boat. When there is more scraping of wood than splashing of water, I stop. I look back. Granddad's cabin is lost in the black outline of the shore.

What the hell am I doing?

As if in answer, the loon howls.

I shiver again. I tell myself it's the cold. My feet and the bottoms of my jeans are soaked, and I'm sweating through my hoodie. Stupid to think I could paddle across the lake, in a leaky boat, in the dark. For what? But ahead the inky silhouettes on Snake Island have shaped themselves into leafy trees.

"It's a Snake Island Adventure." My dead dad's voice. But not just his voice. I see his lips form the words. Giant lips. Hovering over the island. Opening. About to sip from the lake and swallow John Boy. Me. I shut my eyes.

Get a grip.

Splash.

"What the—"

Splash. Splash. Splash.

Every muscle tenses, my breathing stops and my ears tune to the noise.

Splash. Splash. Splash.

Not a fish. A perfect repetitive rhythm. Like my dad swimming.

Shit. I am going crazy.

This isn't a new thought. But my therapist insists the visions and voices of my dead dad are part of "my own unique grieving process."

Splash. Splash. Splash.

Loud and clear and closer.

Refocus your brain my therapist suggested.

Think. Think of something. Anything other than Dead Dad.

Something funny works better. Okay, there was the time John Weaver asked Charlotte Maynard to the prom in the middle of homeroom. The second after the sale of prom tickets was announced on the school's morning news report. Charlotte shook her head no, so fast and so hard, Eli Thompson yelled, "Charlotte. Stop. Remember the butterfly effect. You're setting up hurricanes in the Gulf of Mexico." Now, that was hilarious.

Splash. Splash. Splash.

Shit. I open my eyes and search the lake, but still no moon. I can't see far.

I lunge into the bow, and grab the flashlight. I hit the switch. Nothing. I shake it. Water drips out. "Stupid piece of . . ." I hit the metal side with my palm. It flickers. I hit it again. "Come on." The beam obeys. I aim the pathetic thing at the water and notice—the silence. I swing the feeble rays in a shaky arc. Then I see it and know my therapist is wrong. I must be crazy.

A mermaid. Floating on her back, arms outstretched, in the middle of the lake.

But this is not a Dead Dad vision. I hold the flashlight in my mouth, swallow the metallic taste, and paddle toward the sea nymph.

She lifts her head. "Hi."

I spit out the flashlight. Thud.

Moonlight filters through the edge of the clouds, illuminating my mermaid. But she's not a mermaid. Closer now, I see the blue lenses of her swim goggles pushed up on her forehead. And the turquoise shimmers I thought were mermaid scales are designs on a wet suit. John Boy continues gliding toward her even though I've stopped paddling. Thunk.

She grabs the bow with pale hands. "Drive much."

"Sorry. Not sure where the brakes are," I say.

She tilts her head and grins. "Funny."

I'm glad she thinks so. She's about my age, with a wet braid hanging over her shoulder. Her face is overly round, but two dimples crease her cheeks when she smiles, making me want to smile back. I do.

She taps the boat. "What are you doing? Giving this thing a burial?"

"John Boy's not dead yet."

"If you say so." Another glimpse of her slightly intoxicating dimples.

I look away and glance around, checking for a boat, or another swimmer. "You're not a mermaid, so what are you doing out here alone? There's that rule. Never swim alone." Maybe there should be a never-drive-to-the-pool-alone rule, too.

"I'm not alone. You're here," she says.

"How'd you know I'd be here?" Could I have a mermaid water stalker?

"I saw you from shore doing your sinking, paddling thing."

Her smile drugs me. "So you swam out after me? To save me?"

"No. Don't flatter yourself. I swim to Snake Island and back once a day. But I like night swims better. Fewer boats." She slaps the kayak's hull. "John Boy doesn't really count as a boat."

"You insulting my ride?" I toss back, hoping I sound teasing.

She caresses the tip of the bow, and pouts. "Forgive me, John Boy. I'm sure you can stay afloat long enough to get your captain to shore. I hope."

I hold up the bailing can. "Don't worry. He comes equipped with the latest pump-out device."

Her laugh echoes over the water. "Okay. So you're good then."

I like her laugh. It's bubbly but low pitched—like river water gurgling over rocks, exactly how a mermaid should sound. "You really swim to the island and back alone?"

"Yeah, but my dad usually keeps an eye on me with his binoculars."

"Your dad is watching us?" My voice thins and squeaks on the last word.

"Relax. He's not at the cabin tonight. Just my mom and a couple of her friends, drinking wine and playing cards. I snuck out."

I feel an instant camaraderie. "You must be better at stealth than me. I couldn't make it past my granddad."

She shrugs. "You heard the part about the wine, right?"

"My granddad only drinks coffee."

"Yeah, that's not good. Caffeine gives them hyper-vigilant powers." She laughs.

I don't. The caffeine hadn't worked for my dad.

She gazes past me to the shore. "I should probably get back."

"Yeah, me too."

She points to Snake Island. "Weren't you heading that way?"

"Yeah, but John Boy is leaking pretty bad. I should probably seal the seams with marine putty and try another time." I'm pleased with how impressive my nautical knowledge sounds and "Maybe you'd want to go?" pops out of my mouth.

She pulls herself up on the bow and water rushes over the sides. She lets go and slips back into the water. "John Boy will never hold two of us." She grabs the floating soup can and begins bailing. "We'd need a bigger boat. Or we could swim."

I bail using my cupped hands. Unlike my dad, I'm not much of a swimmer. But I remember the decrepit sailboat not much bigger than a bathtub hanging in Granddad's moldy boathouse. I'd have to climb into the rafters to find the sails my granddad swears are up there. I'd have to battle cobwebs and spiders, which I hate. Between scoops, I sneak a peek at my mermaid. "We could sail there."

"So you've got a sailboat? Is it in as good as shape as John Boy?" She tilts her head. Her thick wet eyelashes clumped together framing her inquiring eyes.

"Probably." I hold my breath, hoping.

"Okay. I'll risk it," she says. "But what's so special about going to the island?"

Would she still want to go when she heard about rotting snakes? I take an exaggerated breath, and imitating my granddad say, "Smell that?"

She breathes in and shakes her head. "No. What?"

I sniff and don't smell anything. I realize I haven't smelled anything foul since pushing off shore. "Forget it. Just my granddad making up stuff." I'd been right. Just an overflowing septic tank, likely Granddad's.

"I'll still go. Sounds like an adventure. By the way, my name's Lana." She lets go of the boat and treads water.

I awkwardly swing John Boy around so I can paddle back beside her. "My name's Dan. Can I ask why you swim to Snake Island and back at night?"

She pulls her goggles over her eyes. "I'm training to swim the English Channel."

I laugh. And either it's the loon, or my dad is laughing too.

Night Probe: The Hermit Crab

Joanne Milavec

If you cannot bear the silence and the darkness, do not go there . . .
—Loren Eisley

Body-soft,
        preferring the tidal pool's gentle wash

you eat from the decay of the earth:
        leaf remnants. Asking for its silence,

                as you pursue life in an abandoned shell
                sunning in a river of stars—

                        your illuminated universe.
A fugitive from the violence
        of daylight and ocean depth. Alive

                to the beckon of night water in shallows.
Your home—a passage allowing curious freedom

                        to live among shape-shifting shadows,
                        in unlit places. Your only enemy:
                        those who mirror yourself.
Lover of the night
        Teach me not to flounder in the velvet wetness
                        and holiness of the dark.

The Missouri Trail

Jan Sparkman

Shakespeare had been in the flowers. The purple and yellow pansies Hope had set out with such pains the day before lay sere and shredded among the scattered mulch. If the dog had been within her grasp at that moment, there's no telling what she might have done. But of course, Shakespeare was nowhere to be seen. If she knew him—and she did—he'd made a dash for the doggie door and his bed beside the water heater in the utility room the minute he heard her car in the driveway. Who could blame him? It wasn't his fault that the yard was not big enough to contain his capacious energy.

She often thought of trying to find him a home in the country, but she had no rural friends who would take him and she found that she could not give him away to strangers. This was his home. No doubt he saw her grandfather's ghost in the narrow garden where the two of them had so often planted shrubs or raked leaves together.

At least his doggie memories were happy. Most of hers were bleak, for her parents had been lonely, dysfunctional people who seemed to find her incomprehensible. She sensed this before she could articulate it, but as surely as she knew it, she also knew that they were as kind and loving to her as they were capable of being. Which wasn't saying a whole lot.

The unremitting sadness of their lives puzzled her all her growing-up years. It wasn't because they were poor, though of course they were. Until Grandpa Lewis died and left her father the house they'd had no place to call their own. On the other hand, they never went hungry. Her father's job was not glamorous, but it paid the bills. What catastrophe had changed them from the smiling, playful parents she dimly remembered from her early years to the morose caretakers of her youth? That mystery held her captive.

The wide front porch was dim and cool. Bordered on both ends with ivy that twined wildly along shabby lattices attached to the roof and shaded on the front by two recalcitrant pines, the porch had been her childhood sanctuary. Now the latticework needed to be torn away before it collapsed under the weight of the matted vines, but the memory of long afternoons spent reading or playing with her dolls under cover of the ivy's dappled shadow had so far kept her from taking any action. She stood there now, forcing herself to see the sagging porch roof, the rotted places in the floor, the furniture's peeling paint. It was obvious that she could not afford to be sentimental much longer.

Inside the house, the phone rang. She fumbled in her purse for the key to the front door, and found it just as the ringing stopped. A telemarketer, probably. It wouldn't be Trent. Not that she wanted it to be, of course. In her saner moments, she was glad that he was not the type to keep calling. After all, she was the one who had broken it off, so talking to him could serve no good purpose. Still, every time the phone rang her heart raced with the expectation that she'd pick up the receiver and hear his voice.

She unlocked the door and stepped inside. She listened, but the whispers and creaks common to old houses were all she heard. Trent had made a habit of leaving the radio on all the time. They'd argued about it—waste of electricity, she said; not enough to matter, he'd said. It was one of a hundred things they'd differed on. It was over and she was glad, but she missed the music.

She kicked off her shoes and padded toward the kitchen to check the answering machine. The light was not flashing, but she punched the 'play' button, anyway, just to be sure. "You have no messages," said an electronic voice.

"I have no life!" She dropped her purse on the table so hard that the vase of fresh daffodils in the center overturned, drenching the linen tablecloth. A word her father would have slapped her for using burst from her lips. She grabbed a dishtowel, but not in time to staunch the stream of water as it poured onto the floor.

A trail of dirt led from the rug beneath the doggie door to the utility room, telling her that Shakespeare was, indeed, inside. When she called his name, he ambled out. From habit, she reached to scratch him between the ears, but she kept her voice stern as she said, "Shakespeare, you ruined my flowerbed!" He merely shook himself, adding to the mess he'd already left on the kitchen's tile floor.

"I can see you're really sorry," she said as she wiped up the water. His blasé demeanor almost made her smile until she thought of the money she'd spent at the nursery and felt like crying instead. Her job as a freelance editor did not give her much financial security.

She got out the broom and dustpan. Might as well clean up the dog's mess while she was at it. Shakespeare lay down on his rug with his head on his paws. Somehow, his total unflappability raised her spirits. She cleaned up the floor and was giving the daffodils fresh water when the phone rang again.

"Are we still on for tonight?" It was Beth.

"Oh," Hope said. "Pizza. I almost forgot."

"You are so out of it, girl. The last thing I said to you this afternoon was 'Meet me at Giovanni's at six.' And you said—"

"I know, I know." Hope tried to sound enthusiastic. "I'll be there, but let's make it six thirty. Okay? I've got a couple things to do before I come."

"Are you all right?"

"I'm fine, but Shakespeare got into the pansies and then he tracked up the floor. I spilled water —"

"Earth-shattering," said Beth.

"Hey, I can do without the quips," Hope said, and it felt good to laugh. "You didn't have to clean it up. And don't worry. I'll be there soon. Oh, by the way, did you call earlier?"

"Nope."

Hope said good-bye, finished the flowers, and went into the bedroom to change her clothes. It was a welcome relief to take off pantyhose and skirt, and get into jeans. Her job as a freelance editor for Hart Publications, a textbook publisher, could usually be done at home from her computer, but now and then she was required to attend editorial meetings at the main office. Today had been one of those days, giving her an opportunity to see Beth who was her liaison with the senior editors at Hart.

Hope ran a pick through her hair and tied it back with a ribbon. She was swiping at her chin with a powder puff when the telephone rang again.

"Hope?" It was a woman's voice, unfamiliar.

"Yes, this is Hope Lewis. May I help you?"

"Hope, it's Emily. Aunt Emily."

It took Hope a moment to remember that this was her mother's sister. One of those not-quite-real relatives she barely remembered. "Aunt Emily? I'm . . . what a surprise! How did you . . . ?"

"Get your number? Oh, I looked it up on the Internet. I just called . . . well, I called earlier. I . . . I'm afraid I have some bad news."

Hope sat down on the bed. "What is it?"

"Mother—your grandmother—died today. You know she had not been well for some time."

Hope hadn't known. How could she? She opened her mouth to ask that question, but Emily was saying, "We thought you should be told."

"Why?"

"Why? I don't understand."

"Why, after all this time?"

Emily was quiet for a moment. "Mother asked us to," she said at last. "At the end . . . she said, 'Don't forget Hope.' We took that to mean that we should contact you."

"Who's we?" Hope knew she was being impolite, but she couldn't stop herself.

"I meant me—and Ardell. Georgia isn't here yet."

"I see."

"We understand that you can't come, of course."

Did they indeed? Anger rushed over Hope like scalding water. She heard herself saying, "Of course I'm coming."

Emily's pause was just a fraction too long. "Yes, do, by all means, if you can get away. I just thought—"

"I'll have to check on planes. I'm not sure about connections to Pitman's Crossing."

"Uh, well . . . Ardell is making arrangements to bury her here in Louisville. At Pleasant Knolls."

"That will make it simpler, then," Hope said, swallowing the harsh words that came to mind at this insult to her grand-mother's country heart. "Just give me the address of the funeral home."

Emily gave it, as well as her own phone number and Ardell's address. Hope wrote them down.

"Everyone is eager to see you, dear," Emily said.

Right, Hope thought, but she let it go. "I'll call when I get there," she said.

After she hung up, Hope went into the living room and sat in the old recliner that had belonged to her grandfather Matt. The sadness that washed over her was totally unexpected, considering the anger she had felt only moments before. It had been more than twenty years since she had seen Grandma Lily. At first, she wrote letters to her grandmother, asking to be allowed to visit when school let out for the summer. She gave these letters to her father to mail on his way to work. He assumed a grave expression before nodding and putting the envelope into his inside pocket. Grandma Lily did not write back. Finally, it dawned on Hope that her father had not mailed the letters she had given him. After that, she just took a stamp from Jonathan's desk when he wasn't looking and posted her next letter, with her return address, on her way to school. Hope expected that Jonathan would refuse to give her Lily's letters if they began to arrive, but when Lily wrote back at once, Jonathan simply handed her the letter with a resigned look.

"Don't tell your mother," he said. By then, Margaret rarely left her bed and took no interest at all in what came in the mail.

When she wrote to her grandmother, Hope renewed her requests for explanations, but Lily ignored them. Her letters were filled with newsy anecdotes of life in Pitman's Crossing, reminiscences of her own parents and grandparents, history in general, or about those long-ago summers with her grand-children. Not once did she address any of Hope's questions. Hope demanded answers from her parents, but was told never to bring up the subject again.

Then Margaret died and Jonathan disappeared even more deeply inside himself than before. Hope devoted herself to her studies, and school became a haven for her. She was surprised to find other young people with similar interests and, for the first time since she had played with her cousins so long ago, she made friends. Her letters to Lily became a forum for writing about all the things she was learning, none of which seemed to be of interest to her father. Her life took on new meaning, and to some degree, she was able to come to terms with her resentment and anger. The pain of the past receded for long periods of time.

Now it all came back. Her grandmother's face swam before her, steady and serene. She saw the summer days of childhood spent playing around the old house at Pitman's Crossing. Those times were etched on her heart in spite of what had happened later. It occurred to Hope that if she went to Louisville, she would see them all—have them all in one place at one time. Someone had to know what had caused the separation between her mother, Margaret, and the sisters she had once seemed to adore.

"I'll make them tell me what happened," she said aloud. That thought energized her.

Giovanni's was crowded, but Beth had managed to secure a spot by the window. "You're only fifteen minutes late," she said as Hope slipped into the booth, "but who's counting?"

"Sorry. I had another phone call just as I was leaving."

Beth gave her a measured glance. "Trent?" she asked.

Hope shook her head. "No. Of course not. I told you that's over."

"I'm convinced," said Beth. "I just wish you were."

"Let's order," Hope said.

"Ooo-kay. Close that subject." Beth's black eyes twinkled.

"My grandmother died. That was the phone call." Hope blurted it out.

"Oh, Hope," Beth touched her hand. "I'm so sorry."

"Thanks. But I haven't seen her for a long time."

"Did she live here in Detroit?"

"Kentucky."

The waitress came and they ordered a large pepperoni with everything.

"Will you be going?"

"To the funeral? I said I would, but it's probably not a good idea."

"Why's that?"

Hope wished she hadn't mentioned it. Now she felt obligated to offer some kind of explanation of her family situation.

"I'm not close to my family," she said.

"I can't imagine." Beth's open face was puzzled.

"Good grief, Beth. Not everyone has your wonderful siblings and—"

"So you're an only child. You've still got family. Everybody does."

"You don't understand."

Beth took a long drink of her soda. "I'm sorry, Hope. It's none of my business."

"Beth, you're my best friend. I'd be glad to tell you. It's just that I don't know what happened myself." She leaned back and closed her eyes for a moment before going on. "We moved to Detroit when I was little. Up until then we lived in a small town in Kentucky about fifty miles from where my grandmother lived in Pitman's Crossing. I used to spend every summer with her. It was the happiest time of my life. My cousins would be there, too, and we would play together all day. At night, Grandma Lily would tell us stories or work puzzles with us, and then we'd go to sleep in big old-fashioned beds with soft mattresses. It was perfect."

"What about your grandfather? Where was he?"

"He drowned when my mother was very young. That's all I know about him."

The waitress came with the pizza and they each took a slice.

"So then what happened?" asked Beth, when she'd finished her first bite.

"That's just it. I don't know. One day my parents threw everything in the car and came here to live with my father's parents. We lost touch with the Kentucky relatives."

"You never visited?"

"No."

"Come on! You never went back?"

Hope shook her head.

"Why do I get the feeling that significant parts of this story are missing?" asked Beth.

Hope shrugged. "On the day we left Kentucky, there was some kind of trouble between my mother and her sisters. A big quarrel. I was there, but nothing they said made any sense to me."

"And no one ever told you what the rift was about?"

"Not a word. I asked over and over, but my parents just stonewalled. After a while, I got the message."

Her father's brooding face rose up before her and she could hear him warning that she'd better not waste her life or she'd be sorry. But he said it the same way he might have said it to the men he sometimes hung out with at Morton's Café, as a way of explaining himself. There had been no sense of companionship between Hope and her father, and after her mother's death he'd become even more distant than before. When he died, she missed his physical presence for a while, but when that went away she felt released.

She was heady with independence—spending her money any way she liked, falling in and out of love, making big decisions without having to run them by her father for approval. But that freedom palled considerably when some of the big decisions turned out to be big mistakes. Trent, for instance.

Hope finished her Coke and got up. "I have to run. I need to call the airlines, do some laundry."

"So you've decided to go?" Beth stood, too, and her round, black face was warm with concern. "Can I do anything to help?"

"No. Yes. Could you feed Shakespeare while I'm gone?"

"No problem."

"Here's my extra key. The food's in the utility room. One big scoop is all he gets. He'll beg for more, but don't give in. And be sure you lock the front gate. I don't want him at large in the neighborhood."

They exchanged brief hugs. "I'll call you when I get back," Hope said. "I won't be gone more than a couple days."

"Take care," said Beth.

That night Hope lay awake a long time, thinking of the past—so clear up to a point and then so murky—and of a future that seemed to hold little beyond the possibility that she might soon have holes in her front porch big enough to fall through.

Shelf Life

Molly Fuller

I say to my friend *Your hair reminds me of the night sky.* I want to say *You are beautiful. Lay off the face paint.* But I know she won't. She makes fat jokes with her body as the punch line.

I have already fucked my eating plan for today by nibbling the edges of this cookie that I snatched off your plate while you weren't looking. Now, I will eat this whole cake that I bought at the cake store on 4th. I would offer you some, but it is one task I have set myself that I plan on completing.

My own body often lets me down. It feels the way I imagine soaking in hydrochloric acid would feel, but I don't actually have an inkling. Did you know that all of our cells regenerate every seven years? I am comforted by this thought: *This particular weariness has an expiration date.*

The Dance

Kathey Schickli

Four a.m.
can't sleep.
Streetlight outside my window
flickers impending death.

Open the door,
paper hasn't come.
Streetlight sighs its last breath and dies.
I look up to mourn for it but see the stars instead.

There's Orion,
I find his belt.
Look north to the Dipper,
suddenly Gemini comes into view.
I twirl like a naughty dancer
barefoot and alive.

a little help

Carroll Grossman

> *"Do not keep needy eyes waiting . . .*
> *do not add to the troubles of an angry mind*
> *nor delay your gift to a beggar.*
> —*Oxford Annotated Bible*, Sirach 4:1–3

"Can you help me," he asks from where he sits on the beach
> "been here three days
> car won't run
> I'm hungry
> I want to go home"
I look at him. I see pale eyes, a pinched face, uncombed hair and
rumpled clothing.
> "Come with me," I say
> up quickly
> wipes sand from his trousers
> walks with me near the water's edge
We enter a restaurant
> "Prepare a sandwich for my friend," I command.
> The cook says, "Ma'am, we see people like him in here
every day."
> "Fix him lunch, son," I reply.
> "It's not like I'm buying him a car."

I Think I Can

Paula Dillmann

I had a strange revelation this week. Here it is: I am exactly the same person I was in kindergarten. Yes, I am bigger and I have a few more credit cards now, but other than that, I am Kindergarten Paula.

I don't know why I didn't see this sooner. I guess years of therapy and doses of philosophy and theology in college made me think I was some complex Jungian / Freudian / Existential / higher-order-thinking being, but no. My development totally stopped at age five.

This is not *Everything I Learned, I Learned in Kindergarten*. This is "Everything I am, I was in kindergarten." Let me explain. Everything I liked about kindergarten, I still like. Everything I didn't like about kindergarten, I still don't like. Everything I did well in kindergarten, I still do well. Everything I did badly in kindergarten, I still do badly. It was all right there in Mrs. Hallman's kindergarten class at Fairport Elementary. I should have just packed it up and never examined my motivations again.

The best part of the day was always the art project. I'm not sure I even remember much else. Surely, there was some mention of numbers, a little science lesson, or hygiene talks. I guess I blocked them out while thinking of the next color crayon I was going to use. I even devised a coloring system all my own. I pressed really hard with the crayon and then scraped off the top layer to reveal a lustrous sheen of color beneath. Next, I went back and outlined the shape, pressing hard to add a touch of drama. If your child should ever undertake such an elaborate and overly time-consuming endeavor in kindergarten, just stop right there and realize that your hopes and dreams of a future engineer are over. In the world of right brain and left brain, you have been given a righty.

Playtime was always disappointing and confusing. There was a large play kitchen in the back of our classroom in which I had zero interest. This explains why I now look for microwave entrees that have only one step. If you have to change the power setting in the middle or turn the entree a quarter of a turn, it's just too much. The cars the boys played with looked like so much more fun, but then you missed out playing with the other girls. Besides, we were all supposed to hate the boys, even though I didn't hate them even then. I look back now and know that the boys were really on to something. Think about it, would you rather drive a sports car or cook? Case closed.

I did like recess, but only because I got to chase my boyfriend, Jerry. I don't mean pursue romantically, like flirt or write notes; I mean I literally chased Jerry. It was probably the only time in my life I have ever run on a playground. To make matters worse, as I chased Jerry I yelled out, "Sweetie Pie Jerry." He ran fast but occasionally looked back and grinned, which was enough to spur me on. In my defense, Jerry was really cute. He was the George Clooney of kindergarten.

I really loved getting in a circle and talking during show-and-tell time, but I was often perplexed by what my fellow kindergartners said. One time we were asked what we wanted to be when we grew up, and all the girls except me said they wanted to be a nurse. I think I almost shouted out, "Hell no!" realizing even then what a tough job that would be. All the boys wanted to be firemen, which I thought sounded way too dangerous, but I did like the idea of the uniforms and riding on the fire truck. My answer? A concert pianist. Never mind that I couldn't play "Chopsticks." It sounded exciting and glamorous. Even then I was slow to grasp the idea of a steady paycheck.

My love of clothes must have started in the womb. I couldn't keep my mind on anything the days I knew Mom was picking me up after kindergarten to go shopping. I was over the moon when I got a fake fur coat and hat to match in a leopard print with black trim. I envisioned hanging it over my coat hook in the big closet we had in our kindergarten room. Everyone in my kindergarten class thought the fur was real. They were a pretty easy audience. Of course, now I still open my closet and see a variety of fake fur coats and vests that make me feel princess-ish, a fifty-two-year-old princess being a scary concept. But the thrill of shopping after school wasn't limited to the high status of fake fur finds. The local five-and-dime, complete with soda fountain, was a treasure trove of shopping, too. I may have been the first to start the high / low fashion-mixing trend. If only I'd had a fashion blog in 1966.

I was the only child of two parents who marched to the beat of a different drummer, so the structure of kindergarten was always puzzling to me. I never had a bedtime and could eat whatever I wanted for breakfast, chocolate cake being my first choice. Thus my kindergarten faux pas weren't intentional, just a result of not being able to understand all the systems. There was a chart for everything. There was a time to get a drink, a time to go to the bathroom, a time to come in from recess, etc. I seldom got into any serious trouble except I did do things at the wrong time occasionally. I went to the bathroom out of turn and I once stayed late on the playground because I was having a good time and didn't notice the bell to come in. I remember getting funny looks from other kids when I didn't follow the rules. Maybe this was the beginning of my life as a Democrat, unable to stay on the straight and narrow. Or possibly, all those other kids are CPAs now. Whatever the cause, my teacher seemed to like me or at least didn't regard me as a kindergarten criminal. She probably just wrote "poor parenting" or "artist" next to my name in her roll book.

My need for comedy and entertainment was also evident in kindergarten. One of my favorite pastimes was the twins. Identical twins with names like Milton and Marvin, and one wore glasses. They liked to switch personalities at recess. One would take off his glasses and give them to his brother, who would then go to the other kindergarten class after recess. This happened periodically and I never tired of it. I always loved when the twin now in my class would pull off his glasses and announce with glee his true identity. I'm not sure the other kids found it as amusing as I did, but for me it was a "ta-da" moment, like seeing a rabbit pulled out of a hat. I can still see them in my mind, looking like Woody Allen must have looked at five—Woody Allen with glasses and Woody Allen without. I'm sure Mrs. Hallman didn't enjoy it at all. She probably wrote "poor parenting" or "comedian" next to his name.

Having a best friend was important to me in kindergarten, too. I'd like to think my friendship with my best friend now is a little more reciprocal than my friendship was with Stacey. I basically decided Stacey was my best friend. She really didn't have any input. I followed her around and told everyone she was my best friend. When we had a project, I got her supplies, too, and made her sit at my table. I sat by her whenever I could and I didn't want her to like the other girls. I can't remember even one time when Stacey talked to me. I think my obsession embarrassed her, but she was too nice to say anything. She probably went home and said to her mother, "That stupid Paula is driving me crazy!" If you're out there, Stacey, I'm sorry and I should have given you some space. I guess I took that kindergarten advice "go make a friend" a little too seriously.

I loved when Mrs. Hallman read a book to us, especially if she let us see the drawings on the pages. A story, then as now, was something I could wrap my head around. The book *The Little Engine that Could* was a particular favorite when the train was trying to get up the hill. "I think I can, I think I can" is really the only motivational phrase that's ever stuck with me. It's probably because I'm still more of an "I *think* I can" person than an "I *can*" kind of person. "I think I can" is not too stressful or boastful. All you are really saying is that you are going to give it your best shot. It wasn't like you *knew* you could, but rather you *thought* you could, and I appreciated the ambiguity and internal struggle in that message. Okay, so I maybe didn't use the words ambiguity and internal struggle, but that's what was going on.

I've decided after all of this that I'm going to quit reading my horoscope, throw away my self-help books, and stop taking *Cosmo* quizzes. I'm going to focus now on what went down in kindergarten. I suggest you do the same. The answers are all there. We just have to look for them. Then maybe we can all reach our full potential. I *think* I can.

Witch Little's Halloween

Charlet Johnson

Witch Horrid locked the door, turned off the lights
She didn't welcome children Halloween night.

Little Witch peered out the window in her room
It's getting dark. They'll be out soon.

She gathered her tutu, ribbons, and lace,
Slipped on her costume, painted her face.

One step, two step, three step, four,
On wobbly legs, she crossed the floor.

Five steps, six steps, and one more,
Turned the knob, opened the door.

"Stop," Witch Horrid's howl rang in her ears
"You can't go out. You must stay here."

"Are you sick? Did you hit your head?
I'll fix you a brew, then put you to bed."

"Your potions, lotions, and witches brew
Will not stop me from what I want to do."

"You're a witch," said Horrid, "no beauty queen.
Covered in scales in an odd shade of green."

Witch Little shrugged her shoulders, turned up her nose
Pranced about on the tips of her toes.

"Going trick-or-treating on Halloween,
Is how this witch wants to be seen?"

She twirled then leapt into the street,
Stopped at each house to ask for a treat.

The other witches gazed out windows and doors,
Straining, craning their necks to see more.

Witch Little returned, holding a bag filled with sweets
Gave each one a handful of treats.

"No one cared. No one stared.
No one ran home scared."

They munched, chomped, smacked their gums,
Stuffed their mouths, spilled not one crumb.

Snaggletooth witches with crooked grins
Wiped sticky, syrupy drool from their chins.

Whispers passed from ear to ear,
"We'll all go trick-or-treating next year."

Time Passages

Maryann Strickland

Through the crisp white wooden screen door, she could hear the sound of the mail truck coming down the street. Its engine revved up and slowed down in a familiar pattern. She listened closely for the door of the mailbox to squeak open and slam shut.

"I'll get it, Mama!" Madeline yelled as her bare feet skipped out the door and across the porch of the beach house. Her footprints followed faithfully behind her in the sand. One outstretched hand slapped against each white board of the picket fence and her blonde curls shone in the sunlight like spun gold as they bounced with each little step. She pulled open the door of the mailbox with a squeak, slammed it shut, and stared at the bent envelope. The letter was addressed to her in red ink. Across the bottom of the envelope in shaky, uneven lettering was the word: "Confidential."

"Mama! Mama! I got a letter," she announced.

"Who's it from?" asked the voice from the kitchen over the clatter of pans rattling.

"I don't know."

"Well, what name is on the return address?"

"There is no name . . . only the initials M. T."

"What's the address?" A hint of impatience crept into her voice.

"It's our address. The return address is our address, Mama."

Mama washed her hands, then dried them on her apron as she came into the living room. "Let me see."

Madeline handed her the envelope. After inspecting it, Mama handed it back.

"Open it, I guess."

Madeline took the bent envelope and slid her finger under the seal and a bit of sand fell out. Side by side, they sat together on the couch and read the words that filled the pages:

A twelve-year-old girl cannot possibly understand which things to pay attention to, which things will have the biggest impact. There are times you will become discouraged. There are sad times ahead, but there are times when you will also experience exhilarating joy. Listen to your Mama.

Your time with her will never be long enough, but her words will guide you long after she is gone, so listen to every one of them. Rascal is the best dog you'll ever have. Treasure every moment. Don't tire of playing fetch with him. Baxter won't play like that and you'll miss it.

Tommy Bishop will steal your first kiss, but don't give him your heart (or anything else). There will be lots of boys who will break your heart before you meet Billy Thompson. You'll be so unsure when he gives you that ring, but when you say yes, that will be one of the best decisions you'll ever make. If Daddy had to give you to anyone else, he would have been reluctant. Billy will make a good father and a wonderful husband. You can count on that.

When the cancer comes and you lose your hair, it will all grow back. You will learn during that period who you can count on. Don't be too mad at little Billy when he wrecks his first car. In time, you will discover that cars can be fixed or replaced and people can't. And when your daughter tells you she is pregnant when she's only seventeen, hold her close. Your first grandbaby will bring more joy into all of your lives than you can ever imagine.

Pay attention to the sounds of the ocean, the feeling of the sunshine as it warms your hair and shoulders, the sound of a loved one's voice calling your name. Do the best you can with what you have. And never leave this place. Home is home, and no matter where you travel and visit and explore, this beach house will always be your favorite place in all the world.

"I'm not sure who this letter was meant for, Madeline, but it does have your name on it. I suppose you can keep it if you like. It is the strangest letter I've ever seen, but it really is most intriguing."

Madeline agreed, then took the letter and put it in the cedar chest at the foot of her bed.

That night when Daddy came home, he kissed Mama with a twinkle in his eye.

"I've brought home a special surprise for Madeline," he announced. "Should I give it to her now or after supper?"

"Now, Daddy! Now!" shouted Madeline.

The excitement in her voice caused the puppy to wriggle out from the box Daddy was holding.

"I guess now," Daddy said with a laugh. "It's a cattle dog. What should we name him?"

"Rascal," said Madeline. "His name is Rascal."

* * *

Sometimes when the moon is full and the tides roll in, and all the conditions are exactly right, unexplainable things can happen. Sacred, mystical things that defy all time and space. A much older version of herself, she sat in her favorite spot on the porch of the weathered beach house, the salty air sticking to her wrinkled skin, the oncoming storm blowing sand across her bare feet. She always loved to be barefoot. The crisp envelope bent beneath her crooked fingers as she laid it on her lap. With a shaky hand, Madeline Thompson reached for the red pen in her dress pocket. She wrote out the familiar address in both the mailing and the return areas. Above the return address, she wrote only her initials: M.T. Across the bottom of the envelope in shaky, uneven lettering she wrote one word: "Confidential."

Nostalgia

María Josefa Reyes

The ocean is trembling on the shore
The sand is moving beneath my feet
And I am delighted because I am alive.
The murmur of the waves pets my ears
As flocks of seagulls
Wake the morning.
The soft kiss of the sun
Touches my skin.
When will I be there again?
I don't know.
My boat stopped on the shore of the river
And now is waiting
To find a good time
To return to the sea.

"Quotation Without Representation"

An Open Letter to People Who Use Unruly Quotation Marks

Erin Fitzgerald

I see you eyeing them—those twists up by the bar.
Lord, you always were a sucker for an easy set of curves.
Do yourself a favor, honey—forget about the ones
holding the Luckies between
come hither fingers,
always batting a thousand
lashes your way.
Sure, they've got the goods—and they'll sell it if you're buying.
"For a limited time only!"
"Buy one, get one free!"
Best to keep your pants on when you jump into that pool, my
        friend.
There's only so far you're gonna float
on borrowed credit.
When the plug is pulled
and the skinny dippers scatter,
you'll be the one left naked, a smoking gun
in your own
hands.
You'll find no trace of *them*
in the foggy morning—
just some lipstick on the mirror.
"Thanks for a good time!"
That's the way with those little flirts.

They may leave you with nothing
but false assurance;
still, they are entitled
to their rightful "final bow."

Time Management for Retired Me

Joan Dubay

Since I retired, I have become interested in using my time in a productive manner. I am not totally inefficient with my time, but there is room for improvement. I bet you I spend at least thirty minutes a day looking for items . . . my shoes, my coffee cup, my glasses. If I count lost thoughts, add another thirty minutes and make that sixty minutes. I am sure I make lists for another ten minutes, so now I am up to seventy minutes.

Hold on—I consider making lists a productive use of my time. I spend less time trying to remember what I wanted to do or what I need to think about when I make a list. So yeah, now I am back to sixty minutes.

My husband tries to help me. *Always put your glasses in the same place. Just sit there until you finish the chapter.* He is an excellent role model, always putting everything in its place. Trouble is, I can't figure out where *his* place is. Like the directions to reprogram the thermostat were above the thermostat on a shelf in a stack of chronologically arranged same issue magazines.

"Why would I look there? How would I find that?" I asked.

"See, it is sticking out," he replied. Just like that made perfect sense. Oh well, we all have our quirks.

I used to waste time trying to find the name of a plumber, or where to put a certain receipt. Now I just place it on a pile and he finds it wherever he finds it or puts it wherever it is he puts it. Our minds don't work the same when it comes time to organizing household paperwork.

Sometimes I ask in a desperate attempt to understand and take some responsibility, "Now where did you put that?" He tells me. I forget by the next time I need it. If I start rearranging a perfectly good system, it will take up another chunk of time doing something I really don't care about and then how will I make time to study Spanish? What's the point of tweaking a system when it will just mess him up? We might risk both not knowing where anything is. All I know is that I am in a heap of trouble if he dies first.

Back to the sixty minutes. Okay, I am going to re-label fifteen of those minutes "making connections." For example, I am in the middle of a home repair project and I suddenly come to a great idea for a volunteer board I serve on. I quickly go to the computer and send off an email. The person whom I emailed happens to be on line and there you go. Did I waste those fifteen minutes? Heck no. I made connections.

That leaves forty-five minutes. My very German father had a work ethic that did not quit. I learned not to waste anything, including time. Our daily ritual was, "What are you going to do today?" and "What did you do today?" Maybe my schedule needs to be tightened up. You remember Wilbur in *Charlotte's Web*? He had a schedule—seven to eight o'clock: talk to Templeton; eight to nine o'clock: nap outdoors in the sun; etc., etc. Wait, I think I'll stop writing and reread the chapter. It was chapter four if you want to read it.

Poor Wilbur, he planned it all out and then it rained. Every day can't be the same, especially when you're retired. Things happen.

Let's see, back to the forty-five minutes. When I worked, I drove about thirty minutes a day. So I will just subtract that thirty minutes from the forty-five minutes and label it "driving" around my home looking for misplaced items and lost thoughts. Now I am down to fifteen minutes. I feel better already.

Anybody is entitled to waste fifteen minutes daily, especially retired me. Problem solved.

The Problem

 30 minutes (looking for items)

 30 minutes (looking for thoughts)

 + 10 minutes (making lists)
  ―――――――――
  70 minutes

 - 10 minutes (reconsidered making lists as a waste of time)
  ――――――――
  60 minutes

 - 15 minutes (affirmed making connections, oh so
  ―――――――――――   valuable)

  45 minutes

 - 30 minutes ("driving" around my home looking for
  ―――――――――――   misplaced items, lost thoughts)

  15 minutes (allotted time to waste)

In the River Valley: Spring

Cynthia Clegg Canada

She stands her ground
against the water that engulfs
her field, her meadow,
her land. When it reaches the boat
tied to the porch rail,
she will consider
paddling downstream to safety.
Until that moment,
she will not waver,
will not bend,
will not surrender.

She knows the river
will win again—it always does.
Still she engages
the perpetual skirmish
against the flood.

The river can take
her pasture, her garden, for now,
but it will give back
generous layers of silt,
rich and fine
to grow more,
                better.

Meantime, she will not bolt
like a skittish mare threatened
by rising currents.
She will watch,
                    and wait
and see that the river pays its due
before it recedes.

Her conviction of the rightness
of giving and taking
will be her redemption.

Pig Pile

Susan E. Lindsey

Porcine papa strolls
Toward sty, sow, and piglets
Brings home the bacon.

Mammoth mama sow,
Her litter piggishly feeds
Pink snouts ecstatic.

Little pig slumbers
Tail spirals over pink spine
Having Charlotte dreams.

The Barbecue King

J. Watson Finger

The screen door slammed on the tightly coiled spring. The pot-bellied man managed to hold the door open with his foot as he carried large crates of ice chunks outside to the restaurant-sized coolers in the shaded area by the trees.

"I told Red that I needed the ice in small sizes; that boy of his must be working at the store this weekend. That boy is not worth a quarter. Takes all day to fill your order and thinks the broom is supposed to sweep the floor by itself. Pitiful," the man grumbled as he stabbed the huge pieces with an ice pick. "If you want something done right, you have to do it yourself."

He paused and looked out onto the busy street. It was a typical Saturday morning. Young pedestrians at the crosswalks impatiently waited to run across the street. Some teenagers did not wait and took their chances dodging oncoming cars. Shoppers quickly walked by with small and large packages of groceries. Truck farmers passed by with a weekend harvest of fresh vegetables to sell. A young boy yelled, "Fresh peaches, tomatoes, green beans, squash, okra!" Another truck with a sign—FRESH FISH—painted on the side door, passed.

"Johnny Lee, your mother talks about you every Wednesday at the sewing circle meeting," an elderly woman said as she stopped to rest in the shaded area. "Sarah tells everybody how proud she is of you. How thankful she is to have a son to come home from the service, from the war. I forget which one, but Sarah is glad to have you back. She said you repaired the roof, fixed the screen door, painted the inside of the house and rounded up workers who were doing all the outside house painting. Yes, sir, your mother is good to have a son such as you. Now, what war did you serve in? World War I?"

"No, ma'am, the Korean War."

"Oh, that's right; you're not old enough for World War I. I get them mixed up. Not much different if you ask me—war is war. Folks shooting and fighting and not getting along. It's all the same."

"Yes, ma'am."

I've got a job waiting on me in Detroit. My buddy Sam said that they were hiring veterans. And Negro veterans have a chance since Harry Truman raised hell with the unions and anybody else. He laughed.

But I had to get tangled up with women and married Rose. Sam mentioned that he could work something out with his boss, but that I needed to make up my mind. There are droves of men traveling from Alabama, Mississippi, and Georgia looking for jobs up North. Detroit, Michigan! Rose doesn't want to leave her family. And Mama don't want to hold me here. But I can't leave her here even though Aunt Minnie and Cousin Georgie live in the neighborhood. I can't just pack up and go, but Detroit! People are making good money up there, opportunities that will never be open here.

"And what's that junk in the back lot?" The woman pointed toward the far corner of the yard. "Johnny Lee, that's not like you to leave things undone."

He turned toward the direction she pointed, stopped, and stared at the large hole. A shovel lay upon a dirt pile. A wheelbarrow was overturned. Other tools were in disarray. Johnny Lee sighed, then shook his head. "That is Wee Willie's hare-brained plan. He thinks that he can show me how barbecue is really done, South Carolina style."

"Wee Willie cook? All I ever knew Elder Claybrook's son-in-law to do is strut around and blow hot air."

"He said that in Carolina, you dig a hole in the ground, start a fire with wood and charcoal, place a hog wrapped in wet burlap on a grate, then cover the hole with the dirt."

"I never heard of such. Looks like he needs a little help. Where is he now? Somewhere chasing a pig?" They both laughed.

Johnny Lee remembered what Elder Claybrook had said to him. "Johnny Lee, you're the son I wish I'd had. My son-in-law means well, but he never finishes anything. Half of the time, I can't understand what he's saying. He gets excited and starts speaking that Geechee singsong talk.

"The Masonic board has agreed that you should run the chapter if I can't," he continued. "The other leaders in larger chapters have heard about you; they are tradesmen who know about jobs close to home. The kind that take you away for a few weeks, but bring you back with heavy pockets. What about that new baby you have? Don't you want to raise him up in a place where he knows his people? The big city is no place to raise a family; it can tear a family apart."

Johnny Lee chewed his cigar nervously.

Rose's family has a special recipe for barbecue sauce, but she doesn't want to share any of it. If her family and I put our heads together, we could make a pretty good business. But those Warfields are a stubborn bunch. They won't give a little to get a little.

"Hey, Johnny Lee! Put me down for five fishplates. I'll send someone for it."

"You got those fires going yet?"

"Been here all night. This is the second go-round."

Men had been stopping over throughout the night, sharing liquor and swapping fish stories, gambling stories, and grand conquest stories. Camaraderie of the fraternity created a no-woman zone.

"You look like you're working hard, Johnny Lee," a passerby said.

"I need you over here. You can always cut some logs, bring some charcoal."

"Sure, can do . . . as soon as I come back from the store with Mary."

"Oh, oh, sounds like you have a few jobs laid out for you," Johnny Lee said.

"Man, you telling me," the man said with a laugh.

The dark man returned to his work, placing the apple wood in the long cement block pit. In the smaller pit, he loaded charcoal in the fire hole. A large kettledrum sat upon three legs under another shade tree.

"What's that, Uncle Johnny?"

"Hey, there. What are you doing sneaking up on me? Are you in the cat business?"

"Cat business?" the little girl asked.

"Yeah, did you ever see a cat walking around and before you know it, it's over in a corner or clear across the room. It walks light and easy."

"I don't watch cats."

"Just people." He smiled.

The smoke traveled in the air, filling the entire area with an intoxicating sweet smell. The smell of grilled meat and enticing spices beckoned customers the entire day. This was the Labor Day weekend, the Masons and Eastern Stars' annual event. The Masonic building was the pride of the community. The front of the building was inscribed:

Mt. Pisgah Lodge No 20

1952 F&AM, PHA. OES Amaranth Ch. 46

RAM Edward Claybrook No. 16

It was a new building, replacing the one built in the 1900s, and it stood as a symbol of the achievements and accomplishments of a prosperous community.

If Elder Claybrook had waited, I would have trimmed the trees on the church property. I was running late, an hour late, helping Cousin Georgie clear the brush in her backyard. I told Elder Claybrook that I would be glad to take care of the church grounds for him. But he has to get up on the ladder and try to do it himself. Now he's got a broken hip. The man was one of the leading founders of our Masonic lodge.

Johnny Lee paused again, turning toward Wee Willie's endeavor. He stared long and hard. *The elder is right. That son-in-law of his has no purpose or conviction. He causes nothing but problems. He tried to charm the Warfield recipe out of Rose and any other family member, and overstepped his bounds. I could stay until*

*the board votes again in the fall, then follow through with those
contacts.*

The little girl coughed.

"You'd better get back; the fire is getting pretty strong. The
other fire is heating up, too. I've got a lot of mutton, chicken,
and pork ribs to cook today," he said, wiping his sweaty face.
His stogie remained in the side of his mouth.

"What's in those pots? And why do you have that rag
stick?"

He picked up the short mop and dipped into the pot. He had
been doing this for as long as the girl could remember, barbecu-
ing for the entire community.

He raised the mop with pride. "Barbecue sauce—mild and
too hot to handle. The kind that will put hair on your chest. You
want to try it?"

The girl shook her head.

"Aunt Rose said that you spend too much time with the
brotherhood."

"Little girl, your Aunt Rose needs . . ." He paused.

"Never mind. You can't always listen to Aunt Rose, nor
repeat everything you hear. You can get into trouble."

"She said if I saw you to tell you that she needed you to
come home."

"Do you want some ice cream? Here take fifty cents and go
down to Buck's and get you something."

He hoisted five large slabs of ribs onto the pit. Opening a
container of lard, he scooped out heaping amounts into the
black kettle. The little girl watched the oil begin to bubble and
dance.

"Get back girl. I'm getting ready to fry." He deftly put the
meal-coated fish into the popping oil.

"Who's going to eat all of that?"

"Anyone who pays for a fish dinner. This will be gone by
one o'clock. All of the buffalo carp, catfish, blue gill, and trout."

"Do you have to go back to the river to get more?"

He laughed out loud. "If I did, I would be sitting there all night long. Fish won't bite when the weather is as hot as today. I've got more in the cooler."

"Aunt Rose said—"

"Girl, it's time for you to get us some ice cream."

Tea Party

Carroll Grossman

The play is not the goal; the goal is to play.
—Dean Young

Twirl my coat round and round and around
wraps and wraps covers my eyes I cannot see
The world spins leaves are blurred strings of green
Arms lift me up swoop, swoop circle
higher and higher fast turn fast turn slow slow
"Faster, faster," I yell. Faster
Not now, time to go inside . . . plop, my feet touch the
    earth.

We go to grandmom's closet mmmn the scent of peppermint
We select, for me, mismatched gloves, long argyle socks
A floppy hat, flowers, antique purse
Wobble in high heel shoes.

Grandmom wears a floppy hat
a long skirt, net stockings, gloves to the elbows . . . no fingers
wobbles in high heel shoes. Finery . . . we are clothed in
    finery
"Look at me," I command. Crinkle, twinkle eyes
I see grandmom . . . She sees me

We pour tea sip extend pinky finger
Napkins on laps a cookie to the mouth munch
        Dainty . . . dainty
        We wipe crumbs from our smiles.

        Stand up. Open arms wide . . . Hold hands
            Ring around the rosie
            Pocket full of posies
            Ashes Ashes We all fall down!

We fall . . . we giggle . . . we hug . . . grandmom and me.

Adverb Lament

Erin Fitzgerald

Verbs rock.
They stomp.
They smash.
They pop.
They *rule*.
But let's not forget one thing. Let's just put it on the table. *Insert*
it there, perhaps.
Verbs *bully*.
They choke, defy mercy.
They lurk,
lure.
They tiptoe up behind
old friends and —
before you know it —
Quickly bolts,
Slowly fades,
Gradually creeps away. . .
like childhood playmates you —
suddenly, unexpectedly —
never
see
again.

All Dressed up with Somewhere to Go

Susan E. Lindsey

In the 1980s, I worked for the phone company. I wore jeans, a leather tool belt, and safety glasses, and wielded needle-nose pliers and a soldering iron in exchange for a paycheck. It wasn't glamorous, but it paid better than clerical work. I stuck with it because I was a single mom with two kids.

I had raised my children by myself since they were three and six. After our divorce, my ex-husband moved to another city, remarried, and liked to pretend that he had no children. Parenting was my job—365 days a year, 24 hours a day.

At home, I was "Mom." At work, I was "one of the guys."

I longed for something in my life that was more feminine, elegant, and refined. I needed to believe that life wouldn't always be like this.

One Saturday in early fall, I went to the local mall to buy a new coat. My kids were hanging out with friends that day. I rarely had time to shop alone, and I was savoring every moment.

I parked near the Bon Marché, part of an upscale department store chain. Clothes at the Bon were typically too expensive for me, but I loved to look. It was unlikely that I would find a practical winter coat there—something indestructible and machine-washable—but I idly slid the hangers along the polished chrome racks anyway.

What I found, what I lusted after, was not at all practical.

It was charcoal gray wool, cut almost like a cloak with sleeves. It had a stand-up collar that extended into a long, trailing scarf; each end of the scarf was tipped with fur—silver foxtails.

I had never wanted a fur coat. My grandmother had a mink stole that she loved; I thought it was silly and pretentious. Full-length fur coats made the slimmest women look puffy and cost more than a perfectly good used car. I had no desire for them.

But this coat pulled me in. I lifted it off the hanger and slid my arms through the sleeves. It was heavy—substantial. I buttoned it up, pulled the collar close to my throat, and flung the long scarf ends over each shoulder. I looked in the three-way mirror, turning to see my back. The wool part of the scarf ends came to my waist; the foxtails extended another foot and a half, ending just above the hem. The coat was beautiful. I felt sophisticated, elegant, and dramatic.

The woman who stared at me from the mirror probably never had to clean up after sick kids, cook macaroni and cheese, or strap on a tool belt. She probably drank champagne at late-evening suppers instead of sitting on the couch wearily folding Star Wars pajamas and watching the eleven o'clock news.

I really wanted that coat. I slipped it off and glanced at the price tag. As I suspected, it was far more than I could afford. I put it back on the hanger, sighed, and headed to Penney's for something practical.

Several weeks later, the kids and I were at the same mall. I again parked near the Bon. I wanted an excuse to walk through that coat department.

As the kids trailed behind me, I walked over to the coats and searched through the racks. The coat was still there—in my size! And best of all, a red sticker now covered part of the tag. The price had been reduced.

I again slid it off the hanger and put it on. My kids stopped squabbling and stared.

"Mom, that's a really pretty coat," my daughter said, petting one of the foxtails.

"Yeah, it's cool," said my son.

My head filled with numbers. I was bone weary of always being practical and frugal. Could I find a way to afford this coat? I hung it back up and we continued our errands in the mall. But thoughts of the coat never left my mind. By the time we were ready to leave, I had decided to buy it. Somehow, I would make the budget work.

The next Sunday, I wore the coat to church. Everyone complimented me on it.

From then on, I wore the coat to church, family events, and on the occasional evenings when I had dinner dates. Whenever I could reasonably assume that the coat was appropriate, I wore it, and I always received compliments.

I felt special in that coat, like a woman who was going somewhere in life.

One Sunday after church, I took my kids and my son's friend to a movie, still dressed in our church clothes. I held my daughter's hand, and my son and his friend walked behind me through the theater lobby. Suddenly, I felt the smallest tug on the scarf around my neck. I glanced back. Each of the boys had picked up a foxtail, and as they walked behind me, they carried them like bridesmaids carrying the bride's train.

My son's friend asked, "Are these real fur?"

"They're fox tails," I responded.

"Did they have to kill the foxes?" he asked.

My son, always ready with a smart remark, said, "No, foxes can live without tails. They can replace them if they go to a retail store." (At that instant, I knew I was out-gunned in the brains department at our house.)

I owned that coat for almost twenty years. My kids grew older. I took advantage of my employer's tuition reimbursement program and returned to college. I graduated with honors and landed professional jobs in big cities. I traveled across the country and to Hong Kong, Paris, Brussels, and London.

I became the type of woman who would own such a coat. I wore it to the ballet, the theatre, elegant dinners, and evening business events.

When I moved to Hawaii from Seattle, I knew the coat would need a new home. Hawaii's warm, humid air and rampant bug population would not be kind to it. I gave the coat to my stepmother. She wore it proudly for a while and then, when I moved to Kentucky, she boxed it up and sent it back to me.

"Winters can be cold in the Ohio Valley. I'm sure you'll find good use for this," her note said. Her note, her love, and the coat warmed me.

I wore the coat a few more seasons and finally sold it at a consignment shop. It was hard to let it go, but I knew it was time. I don't think I ever loved a piece of clothing as much as I loved that coat.

I like to think about the woman who bought it.

Maybe she's a single mom, living on macaroni and cheese, waiting for her next child support check, and shopping at consignment stores. I hope the coat helps her feel warm and secure. I hope she enjoys the drama and attention the coat generates. I hope she looks in the mirror, flips the scarf ends over each shoulder, and smiles at the elegant, confident woman she sees.

Loss

Cynthia Clegg Canada

A heart touched once
is forever changed.
You cannot
un-touch.

Paths that cross
do not un-cross;
not remembered
is not the same as
forgotten.

Friends not called to mind
are still beloved
after years
of quietly sitting
in the corners
of memory's attic,
saying nothing—
just
occasionally
smiling.

And when a friend
steps down from the attic
only to say,
I have left this Earth,

the gap is as real,
the hurt as sharp,
his corner as desolate
as if you'd seen him
just this morning,

Fit as a fiddle,
Right as rain.

Wellspring

Holly Hinson

I knew not how to survive
the parched lips of his grudging affection

Clinging to the barest sustenance, he dispensed for my daily
bread
So spare I no longer share its meagerness
Mercifully, it ended
I was alone
Falling away into hollow

A long slow climb out of a penniless well
My heart cleaved in two
My fingertips chalky, bloody
from scaling the sides
one block at a time

After a long and barren solstice,
so long it took a second glance to notice
You—a flash of moment
a quickening of blood
a glimpse of newfound faith
Your kindness a tonic in my soul

I knew not how to survive
perched on this precipice

Unrequited longing
Unfinished tears
caught aching in my throat

can now rush forth
dried by the heat of a new naked kiss upon my temple

first a sigh of relief
a budding smile
and then my joy broke open
an urn crashing on cobblestone
spilling love into your garden

Stretching in the sky, the trees watch over our love
It is small and humble but mighty

I am awash in amazement
Through the dusty window you saw

So clearly, so unreservedly,
the very nature of my need
when I couldn't even fathom it myself

How could you?

For so many moons, I was underground

Now I am unearthed
discovered
beloved

Life on the Inside
Jeannie Waldridge

The last time I saw my mama was inside the Alabama State Department of Corrections. Well, the last time I saw her in person. I was about eight years old and taken there by my foster mom, Arnetta, and my social worker, but I can't remember her name. At the time, it was a state rule that all children having their parental rights terminated could visit with their parents for one hour to say their good-byes. As long as there were no prison problems, the judge would make the social worker have the visit there in a special family room.

I don't really remember much about that day; I hadn't seen my mother since I was a little kid. She looked much older. Her tight-fitting, fancy, sparkling clothes and painted nails had been traded in for loose-fitting khaki pants and shirt and short trimmed fingernails. This woman had become almost unrecognizable. Before I left, she stuffed a folded piece of paper inside my jacket pocket. My eyes burned a little when my mom leaned down and kissed me on the cheek and whispered, "You're a young lady now and young ladies do not cry." Her eyes were red and swollen and began to fill with tears. Walking out of those gates, I looked back and I no longer saw my mama. I simply saw State Inmate #F72324. I promised myself that I would never return to such a horrible place and I made sure I didn't cry.

I kept my hand in my pocket and held the little piece of paper tight. Now, some people would start to feel sorry for me. You know, those goodie-two-shoes white folks who are always looking for some charity case. I have never needed anyone to feel sorry for me. That social worker, she knew I was strong, too. After that day at the prison, I never saw her again.

I stayed at Arnetta's house until the summer of my eighteenth birthday. Arnetta needed to make room for another foster kid so she could pay her bills. She helped me pack my bags and sent me on my way and I made sure I didn't cry. I was the only student to arrive at college with two black garbage bags, a small canvas tote, and a fading crumpled note. The holidays were usually the loneliest. I would always make sure I scheduled myself to work so I had an excuse to remain in town and in my room. My old foster mom, Arnetta, was busy with her new family and her sporadic phone calls eventually stopped.

From time to time, I would find myself sitting at the computer feeling sorry for myself and a little lost. I would reach for the crumpled piece of paper, go to the Alabama State Department of Corrections website, and type in "Inmate #F72324." Looking past the graying hair and slight weight gain, I would find the eyes of my mother. It always seemed odd to me that though she remained locked up, her eyes and her spirit seemed free. In those eyes, it always felt like home. A place that said I belonged; that I have history and that somewhere I do have family. Those late nights spent staring at the computer were the closest I ever came to crying.

The years passed and I eventually settled down with a nice man. He was not handsome, but he was a good provider and was very loyal. The day we found out we were pregnant was the day I was finally able to throw away the torn and tattered piece of paper. The words on the page had almost totally faded. But I could still read "Alabama State Department of Corrections, Inmate #F72324, Love Always, Mama." The rest of the words no longer mattered and I was no longer defined by my mother's choices or a crumpled-up piece of paper. It was the happiest day of my life, and I didn't cry.

Yesterday

Kathey Schickli

the sun danced its way through the branches of the tree,
long shadows tumbled softly across the path.
I walked home through the side yard
surprised to find you there

on your knees, humming softly under your breath,
a lullaby I had not heard in years.
The memory of it stopped me. I smiled
as you hammered away on that old bird house

in your faded blue shirt, the one you always wear
when serious work has to be done.
You, mender of things broken, you,
who knows exactly the right salve

to repair a broken heart, to heal a wounded soul
when no one else sees the need.
I tiptoed away so I would not disturb you there—
on your knees—softly humming that lullaby.

Ending Graces

Margaret F. Grimes

The service ended with a familiar hymn. We all filed out of the Congregational church to greet attendees on the lawn. The New England summer sun felt warm and soothing. The few people who came were among the old residents who knew her years ago. The headmaster from the prep school where she had taught, and some faculty members were also there. The sparse number was not a surprise. She had been in a nursing home, out of state, a long time. Forgotten.

Her son and daughter were there greeting people, polite, but without tears. Theirs was an air of tolerance for the rituals of a funeral, not grief. Some of the grandchildren were restless to get this over, pacing, slapping hands over quiet jokes, and laughing . . . too old to display this behavior so openly. There seemed no feeling of loss among them. The polite gestures and handshakes from attendees prompted extended comments of reacquaintance with their condolences. This was taking longer than expected.

I was there because I loved her. She was my aunt who had provided family summers on the farm with freedom, picnics, intelligent advice, and comfort when I rebelled against my father. My handkerchief was wet, eyes swollen. I stood to one side to collect myself. There was no hurry. My cousins ignored me; few people acknowledged me. They didn't remember me either. But I was there to see her to her final rest, bid my own good-bye, and would not leave it incomplete.

A well-dressed young man stood alone on the fringe of the crowd, waiting his turn to speak to someone from the family. No one made an effort to include him. I stepped over to greet him, and said I was her niece, that she was very dear to me. I appreciated his coming. My emotion was clearly visible.

As he shook my hand, it lingered just a moment as he introduced himself. I recognized his name as that of a famous professional racecar driver she had mentioned. He had come often to see her at her house; took her out in his sports car to lunch with his mother. He said he wanted to tell someone how special she was to him with a little story.

When he was in prep school, she was his art teacher. She had encouraged him to explore his creative juices, awakened a love of art, and discovered a hidden talent. In addition to racing cars, he now was also an artist, had had several exhibitions, and was selling his work. I told him that was wonderful to know. She would be pleased. He said she already knew it. He had even sent her one of his paintings, but that was not the story he wanted to tell.

Because of his love of cars, and desire to race them, his mother had built a full-sized practice racetrack for him on their farm near the Lime Rock Racetrack. He could drive all he wanted on their private property way before he was old enough to have a license. Everyone at school knew this. It was a constant on his mind.

While in school, his sixteenth birthday fell in the middle of the week and he could not leave campus until the weekend. Mrs. T. called him to her classroom and said, "Come with me."

"She drove me down to the town hall to get my driver's license, and paid for it. She knew it was an important day. When we came out with the treasured prize, she handed me the keys to her car and said, 'Now you drive us back to school . . . the long way.' It meant the world to me to be so trusted as a sixteen-year-old, even to risk breaking school rules on that important day. I have never forgotten it. I just wanted someone to know how really special she was."

He made his way to shake hands with my cousins, then left.

After the burial, there was a family lunch. In the conversation, I mentioned who he was and what he had said to me. This should be shared within the family. They all swarmed around for more detail about him, where he raced, why hadn't I brought him to their attention, asked this question or that. *Of course*, they knew his famous name, but it had not registered in the fog of formality.

Clearly, they also missed the point.

Sanctuary

Holly Hinson

You opened your red door, your sacred space
Invited me

I hobbled in, wounded, cynical

You opened your harvest heart, made space
I curled up, nested in your warm chamber

Waited for the other shoe to drop
Watched, wistful

Your welcoming soul
Sought connection—communion—fierceness—fire

I buffered myself, waiting for a storm that didn't come
And almost missed the sun

You opened your eyes and saw through
saw who
saw abundance and beauty
and lifted me up to bask in my bliss

You opened your arms
I fell into the hundred thousand wells of your love—
Surrendered all pretense

Patchwork Quilt

Maryann Strickland

Everywhere she went
People turned their heads to look at her
A patchwork quilt
She was made up of all of the people who had ever touched her
life
And she wore little pieces of them
Wherever she went
And all could see
How much
And how deeply she had loved
For each one was so intricately sewn into her life
And she wore them wrapped around her like a blanket
For all the world to see
Until they became a part of her
And it was impossible to see
Where one ended
And the other began

Hilarye's Home

Jeannie Waldridge

The last place she thought she would find herself was living back in her parents' house. Thirty years ago, when she left at eighteen, she had no intention of ever coming back.

Her life there had been pure hell and she believed anything and anywhere would be better than staying. She had managed to stay away until she received the call that her father had died. That was almost a year ago and she had not found the courage or the strength to leave. The guilt of leaving her mother alone far outweighed her desire to get out of town.

Hilarye had managed to find a job as a photographer at a local newspaper. She loved the excitement of the chase, and it allowed her an opportunity to escape her own miserable life. Somehow, taking pictures of other people's tragedies made her feel better.

Some days, Hilarye felt so trapped she found it hard to catch her breath. She worked full-time, handled the household chores, and took on the daunting task of caring for her dying mother. At times, it was overwhelming. Her mom had been released from the hospital two weeks earlier. Now she had to work her schedule around the hospice nurses and care providers.

On good nights, Hilarye and her mom would sit up for hours. Her mom talked almost non-stop. It was as if she had thirty years' worth of conversations that she was trying to squeeze into her last few months. It was odd; after years of living practically as strangers, Hilarye found they had many things in common. A love of trashy romance novels, a warm cup of

French vanilla coffee, *I Love Lucy* re-runs, and fancy gardening magazines.

Often, Hilarye would find herself sitting in the sunroom, staring at family pictures hanging on the wood-paneled walls. Even after all these years, her father's empty stare would almost pierce her skin as he glared from the boundaries of the plastic frames. Hilarye never felt like she was good enough. He was tough and heavy-handed in his child rearing.

"Spare the rod and spoil the child," he often said during the arguments he had with Hilarye's mother when she tried to intervene. Hilarye resented her mother for not packing up and leaving him. That just wasn't done back then. Women stayed and made the best of it, no matter how bad *it* became.

Hilarye arrived home one afternoon to find her mother sitting on the sun porch, sipping coffee and chatting with her care provider. She saw her through the picture window as she parked the car along the street. Her mother was always a great storyteller. She threw her head back, her eyes shut tight, and she covered her mouth as she laughed endlessly. As Hilarye walked in, her mother nudged the care provider.

"See, isn't she beautiful? That is why we only had one, stopped with perfection." Her mother softly smiled and winked. Hilarye grinned and remained speechless. She stood in the doorway like an awkward fifth grader who had just been awarded the grand prize in the spelling bee.

Weeks passed. After hearing a light thump outside, Hilarye walked to the front door and opened it slowly. Wind and snow swirled and the cold lashed her cheeks. By her feet, she discovered a small pot with tiny white flowers. She recognized it immediately as a *Galanthus nivalis* or the more common name, snowdrop. Footprints in the snow led to and from the porch, and a note tied to the slender stalk fluttered in the icy air. She never heard the delivery driver knock even though she had left clear instructions since the doorbell did not work. *I really need to get the doorbell fixed*, she thought. Hilarye had ordered the flower weeks ago from Daniel's Florist. He had warned her it would take a while since they would have to be special shipped from Europe. Her mom had become fascinated by the flower when she was reading a romance book series with a heroine named Snowdrop. When the hospice nurse began to discuss the looming options for her mom, Hilarye became obsessed with getting her some snowdrops.

She bent down and picked up the pot, held it close to her nose, and breathed in deeply, then quickly shut the door. She wasn't sure if it was an effect of the door being opened, but she suddenly felt a cold chill and goose bumps formed on her arms. Hilarye glanced around the room and located the perfect spot. She smelled the flowers again as she walked across the room towards the sun porch. The honey scent quickly filled the air. She glanced out the window to the spot where she had stood weeks earlier and seen her mother so happy. Slowly she eased into her mother's chair, picked up her cup of coffee, and arranged the flower on the table next to her mom's empty cup.

For the first time, Hilarye felt at peace. She found it ironic that after so many years of running she would end up in this house and under the watchful eye of her father. Caught up in the excitement of the flowers' arrival, she anxiously called out for her mother. The silence reminded Hilarye she was once again alone. But this time, she was no longer running.

Infinity

Cynthia Clegg Canada

When I was seven
or eight, I would lie awake
stretching my mind's eye
to see the edge of
the universe. What lay
on the other side?
For that matter, what
marked the border? Fence? Wall? Field
of impenetrable
energy? Maybe
a path of intergalactic
stepping-stones.

Last Rites

J. Watson Finger

"Onward, Christian soldiers, marching as to war," the frail voice sang. The beeping sound of the monitor kept time with the singer, or so it seemed. The raspy breathing of the singer returned. A nurse whisked into the room, adjusted the machine, then disappeared. The sound of her squeaky shoes lingered outside the room.

"With the cross of Jesus going on before."

* * *

The morning mist dripped on the kitchen window. "Umm, my kind of morning, nippy." The tall man put the old aluminum coffeepot on the wood-burning stove at exactly four a.m. He let the coffee perk for a good ten minutes, so it would be strong and black. He fried two eggs for himself, fried large slabs of job bacon in another skillet.

"This pot of oatmeal will hold the children through the morning," he said and he pushed the pot to the back burner. "Homemade bread is better the next day," he continued, as he sliced the bread for toast. "The children can eat the rest." Finishing his breakfast, he walked toward the hallway and bellowed, "Rise and shine, children!" He reached for the large black hat he called Jack Swan. "Old Jack Swan does the trick every time," he chuckled, as he placed the hat on his head. Tales of a father's make-believe bad man brought frightened looks to the children's faces whenever he threatened to take the hat from its place on the wall.

* * *

Slits of light were cast upon the bedcover. The woman in pink opened the venetian blind. More light revealed another woman sitting in the corner. She sniffed quietly into the Kleenex.

"Joshua fit the battle of Jericho, Jericho, Jericho," the old man's voice boomed. "And the walls come tumbling down!"

"Why does he keep singing those songs? I never knew him to sing."

"The nurses said that he's been singing throughout the night."

"Can't they give him something?"

"The nurses will take care of it. Maybe you should go back to the house and get some rest. I will call you if there's any change. There's not much we can do, just keep Daddy comfortable."

The patient's labored breathing interrupted the silence in the room. The door opened again.

"Good morning, daughters," whispered the priest. "Mr. Rob is one of our most devoted parishioners. We aren't a big church, but our faith is large and the Holy Spirit keeps us afloat. It has allowed Mr. Rob to do good works for the church. Once he has passed, the church will need fifty dollars to pray his soul out of purgatory."

"Humph."

The priest asked, "Do you think the family can pay for his soul? The church doesn't have a charity fund."

"He's been in the hospital for a week and now he gets noticed?"

"Calm down, Carman. Father, we appreciate your visit," the calmer sister replied.

"I don't know why he decided to leave the Baptist church in the first place," the distraught sister sniffed. "Our family has been Baptist for many generations."

"Daughter, Mr. Rob came to us when he stopped drinking."

"When was that? I don't remember my father ever taking a drop. As much as he worked at that church. He'll never get out of purgatory if I have anything to do with it. I'm not giving you one red cent!" She began to cry.

The priest's face turned a deep red.

"Daughter, the church loved Mr. Rob. He was one of the best of the flock. Folks in the community comment on our flower beds, our thriving vegetable garden brings a profit at our summer fair, and Mr. Rob made many improvements to our little church."

"Somebody's knocking at your door. Somebody's knocking at your door. O sinner, why don't you answer?"

The light in the room changed.

* * *

"Sweet Pea, you go home and bring the wagon to Johnston Meat Packing Warehouse." The young girl returned, pulling the wooden wagon. Her father filled it with large packages of slab bacon, bologna, ham hocks, and two smoked hams.

"You go straight home with this, girl. Don't idle; plenty folk will want what you have. Mr. Johnston and I worked out a bargain. I guard the warehouse and get as much meat as I want along with my pay."

* * *

"Sweet Pea? Sweet Pea?" the old man called, patting the hospital sheet. "What's that? She's talking too loud. My girls, my girls, they mean well, but never listen. Be still, daughters."

"Someone's crying Lord, kumbayah; someone's crying Lord, kumbayah."

The noonday light penetrated the room.

* * *

"Climbing this ladder ain't what it used to be, but if I get up on the roof before midday, I can take a rest afterwards. I promised Father Temple that I would find the leak and tar it today." He took another step, and then paused before landing on the roof.

"*Rob Hays, why are you on that roof? You don't need to be up there at your age. It's too hot and too dangerous,*" his daughter chided.

"*All right, daughter; no need to carry on. Don't you have a family to take care of?*"

"*This church will be the death of you.*"

* * *

At the small funeral, an angelic choir of three sang Mr. Rob out of Purgatory. He was buried in the small Catholic graveyard that he had so dutifully tended. His family had acceded reluctantly to his last wish, and the weather-beaten priest found a reason to pray for Mr. Rob's soul.

Notes on Contest Winners

Tabatha Hibbs, author of the first-place story, "Foot Washing," currently lives in Tahlequah, Oklahoma, with her husband, herd of cats, dog, and dragon. She writes fiction and poetry, as well as scholarly essays on objects and noise in British modernist literature. She is also developing a freshman composition textbook that focuses on developing research writing skills. Hibbs received her PhD from University of Tulsa and teaches freshman composition and humanities at Connors State College. Her work has appeared in *Words, Words, Words* and in *Broad River Review*.

Gwen Hart, author of the second-place story, "This is a Good Idea," teaches English at Buena Vista University. Her poems have appeared in literary journals such as *Lake Effect*, *MARGIE*, and *The Formalist*. Her book of poetry, *Lost and Found*, is available from David Robert books. She lives in Storm Lake, Iowa, with her husband, Roger Hart, a fiction writer, and more than 250 pounds of Newfoundland dogs.

Suzanne Purvis, author of the third-place story, "Paddle Through," is by day a wife and mother to two teenagers, and underling to two dogs. By night, she is a blogger, a successful writer of short fiction, and an aspiring novelist. Purvis has won awards for her short fiction including the University of Toronto Trinity College Short Fiction Contest and Romance Writers of America Launch a Star Contest. "I am a huge football fan," she says. "I love the beach in the winter. Small rodents freak me out. My favorite holiday is April Fool's Day and it just happens my son was born on that day. My favorite color is lime green, but not to wear. My favorite food is popcorn, but I rarely get it at the movie theatre. I'm adding yoga to my life, but I won't attempt a headstand. And I still love going and hanging out in the children's section of the library." Purvis lives in Niceville, Florida.

Jan Sparkman received honorable mention for "The Missouri Trail," an excerpt from a novel in progress. Sparkman earned her bachelor of arts in writing and literature from Burlington College, Burlington, Vermont, and has also studied at Sue Bennett College, London, Kentucky; Cerritos College, Norwalk, California; University of Kentucky, Lexington; and at Eastern Kentucky University in Richmond. She has been a self-employed writer since 1972. From 1990 to 1997, Sparkman worked for the *Laurel News Leader*, in London, Kentucky, doing a biweekly column, copyediting, ad design, layout, feature stories, and office management. Sparkman has served on the boards of two literary entities in her area and has facilitated the meetings of a bimonthly writers group for a dozen years. She lives in London, Kentucky.

Selene G. Phillips, Wabigonikewikwe, is a member of the Lac du Flambeau Band of Lake Superior Ojibwe Nation of Wisconsin and an assistant professor at the University of Louisville. She teaches journalism, Native American courses and performs Chautauquas as Sacagawea and Mary Todd Lincoln. Her PhD is in American studies from Purdue University, as is her BA in science/sports movement and radio/ TV. Her master's is from Indiana University.

Her poem, "ceremonial death dance," appears in *Yukhika-latuhse?* Her book chapters appear in several outlets: "Indians on our Warpath: WWII Images of American Indians in *Life* Magazine" in *American Indians and the Media*; "Sacagawea: Super Hero, Super Woman, Super Myth" in *American Indians and Popular Culture*; and "Surviving Cultural Suppression: Sharing and Transferring Ojibwe Identity in Lac du Flambeau," in *From Generation to Generation*.

She belongs to the honor society of Phi Kappa Phi; the Society of Professional Journalists; the American Journalism Historians Association; the Native American Indian Studies Association; the Indigenous Professors Association; the American Studies Association; the National Communication Association; and the Southern States Communication Association.

Phillips enjoys outdoor sports; especially ice skating, snow-shoeing, cross country skiing, water skiing and swimming. She loves water, even when frozen.

Harriet L. Shenkman, PhD, received second-place honors for her poem "The Possibility of Teetering." Shenkman is a professor emerita at City University of New York. She serves on the advisory board of the Women's National Book Association, NYC. She was awarded second place in poetry in the Women's National Book Association National Writing Contest, 2013. She is proud to serve as poet-in-residence at BoomerCafe.com and to have a poetry page on VerseWrights.com. Her poems have been published in a number of publications and she is working on a poetry collection, *Sweet and Sour Soup.* She is also completing a novel entitled *The Camel Tamer*. Shenkman lives in New York with her husband Jerry; they have three children.

Joanne Milavec wrote the third-place poetry entry, "Night Probe: The Hermit Crab." Milavec has been writing as long as she can remember. Her career has been in teaching English from second grade through college. "I hope I have instilled in my students my twin loves: reading and writing," she says. "These interests are based on a fascination with new experiences and a love of language." Milavec has been published in *Pinyon, Kalliope, Progenitor,* and *Winning Writers.*

Molly Fuller's poem "Shelf Life" received honorable mention. Fuller earned her master of arts from Ohio University and her master in fine arts from Sarah Lawrence College. She is currently a visiting assistant professor at Marshall University. Her work has appeared in or is forthcoming in *Hot Metal Bridge*, *Quickly*, *Crack the Spine*, and *Potomac*. She divides her time between West Virginia and Ohio.

Notes on Contributing Members

Cynthia Clegg Canada has been a member of Women Who Write for five years and edits the monthly newsletter, *The Writers' Wire*. She has been telling stories for as long as she can remember. She has published a handful of short stories, several freelance newspaper articles, and a poem or two. Canada considers herself an author of short fiction and essays, having worked hard to develop the craft of pretty good prose. Having long ago determined that her own poetry is mostly hyperbolic prose with funny spacing, she has, nevertheless, in the last couple of years, taken her first running leaps at poetry in about three decades. She believes that when poetry happens to her, it's because Something Bigger passed it on. She's just the messenger.

Paula Dillmann is a retired art teacher, whose twenty-two years of teaching middle school have fine-tuned her sense of humor and enabled her to write crazy things. She has had poetry published in *LEO* magazine and was a Louisville Writing Project Fellow. She has degrees from Bellarmine University, the University of Louisville, and Indiana Wesleyan University.

Joan Dubay is a recently retired primary school teacher. Writing is only one of her new endeavors.

J. Watson Finger is a former educator and University of Louisville instructor, and has worked for the *Washington Post* and the *New York Times*. She has had articles published in *University of Louisville* magazine and the *Louisville Defender* newspaper, and has presented workshops at the University of

Louisville. She also developed a women writers' program at the Louisville Newburg Library. She is a current member of the National Trust for Historic Preservation and the Kentucky Historical Society, and has participated as a diversity scholar. She is also a visual artist and has exhibited with the Kentucky Coalition for African American Arts throughout the tri-state area. She created and coordinated the H. L. Neblett Historical Quilt Show in Western Kentucky. Finger also appears as a member of the Montage artists' organization in *Two Centuries of Black Louisville*. She is presently working on a children's novel and an anthology.

Erin Fitzgerald is a community arts enthusiast and equal opportunity writer. Her work has been included in various publications, such as volumes 2 and 3 of the *Motif* series by MotesBooks, *The Single Hound*, *Literary LEO*, and *New Southerner*. She placed third in the 2013 Lincoln Memorial University Mountain Heritage Literary Festival writing competition (Jesse Stuart Prize for Young Adult Fiction) for her story "All Fall Down." Fitzgerald is also a singer-songwriter and plays in numerous music groups, as well as solo, in styles ranging from traditional to rockabilly to punk. Fitzgerald lives in Louisville, Kentucky, with her brilliant children who inspire her every day.

Margaret F. Grimes is a freelance writer and memoirist, currently residing in Louisville, Kentucky. Language and writing have been her passion all her life. She has previously contributed articles and short prose to publications as a language teacher, marketing and promotions manager, and as a development officer. Her most recent publication is a memoir entitled *Summer Tales: Memories of a Southern Girl in Yankee Land*, a collection of stories from an unusual childhood. She is currently working on a historical novel.

Carroll Grossman, also known as Teaberry, is a teacher, speech-language pathologist, and writer who lives and works in Louisville, Kentucky. Born and raised in the mountains of Eastern Kentucky, she learned early on to follow her dad along narrow deer paths, steep hills, and razorback ridges, and across clear, cool streams. She realized later that the trees she found so big and sometimes scary as a child, really were grand. The woods she walked with her father, a forest-fire spotter, are part of Blanton Forest, an old-growth forest. Her many hours spent wandering in the hills and creeks of Eastern Kentucky left an enduring love of the out-of-doors and a passion for preserving the beauty and natural resources in Kentucky. Many of her stories and poems reflect the honest, strong, and complex character of those living in economic poverty surrounded by mountains big enough to slow the sunrise. Grossman's work has previously appeared in *Edible Louisville* and in the 2011 and 2012 editions of *Calliope*. Her first book, *Possibility . . . yes,* was published in 2012. She is a founding member of the Cherokee Roundtable, a group of local writers who meet regularly to share current writing.

Holly Hinson is a storyteller, poet, mom, and grandma, avid nature lover, spiritual seeker, and proud Episcopalian. She is a member of Women Who Write, and a features writer and marketing and communications coordinator for KentuckyOne Health at the University of Louisville Hospital and the James Graham Brown Cancer Center. She is also a freelance writer for Jewish Community Center and other publications. A lover of blues music, dancing, performing arts, diverse neighborhoods and wonderful parks, Hinson believes Louisville is a great place to call home.

Charlet Hanna Johnson, author of "Witch Little's Halloween," became hooked on writing after taking classes offered through Metro Parks. She also took three writing courses with the Institute of Children's Literature. At the time, Johnson was working for the Jefferson County Board of Education Food Service. She approached the school's principal and suggested a read-aloud section in the school letter, and then published short stories and poetry in the Johnsontown Elementary School monthly newsletter. Since 2000, Johnson has worked at the j.camille cultural academy, sponsor of the annual Children's Picture Book Writing Workshop and Write for Children and Teens: Stepwise Program.

Susan E. Lindsey is a writer, book editor, and former newspaper columnist. Her work has appeared in *Underwired* magazine, the *Calliope* anthologies, the *Highlander* newspaper, and on RaphaelsVillage.com. She has won or placed in various national, regional, and local writing competitions. Lindsey is a recipient of a 2012 artist's enrichment grant from the Kentucky Foundation for Women in support of her historical nonfiction book in progress. Lindsey worked in corporate communication and public relations for nearly twenty years before launching her own company, Savvy Communication LLC (www.savvy-comm.com). She is director of Louisville-based Women Who Write, and a member of the American Copy Editors Society, the Editorial Freelancers Association, the Talking Story writers group, and numerous historical and genealogical societies. Lindsey has taught at the Carnegie Center for Literacy and Learning in Lexington, Kentucky, and frequently speaks to writers about writing and editing.

María Josefa Reyes was born in Holguín, Cuba, in 1954. She lives in Louisville, Kentucky, where she obtained her American citizenship, and earned a master of arts in education at the

University of Louisville. She teaches Spanish for Jefferson County Public Schools. She is a member of the Louisville Writing Project, the National Writing Project, and Women Who Write. Reyes was featured in a May 8, 2000, Louisville *Courier-Journal* article about her life and work. In Cuba, she taught Spanish and literature at the secondary level, and was literary advisor at the Velasco Cultural House. She has contributed poems and articles to Cuban and foreign magazines and the Cuban newspaper *Ahora*. Her work was also published in the *Anthology Fiesta de espinelas*. She received two awards in Cuba's Rubén Martínez Villena national literary contest: first place in children's literature for *Las vacaciones de Marisol* (1997) and in the poetry division in 1996. Her poems have been included in several collections of Cuban poetry. *Marisol's Vacation* includes poetry and stories for children, and *Andar la ternura* and *Vuelo de guitarras* are Spanish books of poetry for adults. Her work has previously appeared in *Calliope*.

Kathey Schickli is a native of Louisville, Kentucky, who began her career as a schoolteacher in Jefferson County, Kentucky. While working at JCPS, she also served as a curriculum writer and editor for independent study courses. After teaching for seven years, Schickli pursued her interest in art and design, earning a post-baccalaureate degree in art and interior architecture. She started her own commercial design firm specializing in healthcare facilities. She has had numerous articles published on the environmental impact of new products and manufacturing techniques in the marketplace. Schickli has always had a passion for writing and especially enjoys writing poetry about moments of epiphany in everyday life. She has two daughters and a granddaughter.

Maryann Strickland was taught by her mother to read when she was just two years old. Reading and writing have always been a part of her life that brought great joy—and provided a way to escape to other worlds for adventure and respite. Strickland is a supervisor for Child Protective Services in Jefferson County, Kentucky, where she has worked for eighteen years. Her work with diverse populations, families in crisis, and intensely sobering situations has helped her develop an enthusiasm for life, a sense of humor, a positive attitude, and a sense of what is important in life. Strickland has been published in the *'Ville Voice* and *Home for the Holidays: Stories and Recipes.* She is currently working on a collection of inspirational writings.

Jeannie Waldridge is originally from the small town of Harrodsburg, Kentucky, but has lived in Louisville for the past thirteen years. She is a certified alcohol and drug counselor, and she currently works for the Kentucky Department of Corrections as a program administrator. She has had a lifelong passion for humorous storytelling and is beginning to translate that love into her written works. She is currently working on a children's novel and short stories.

Books available from Women Who Write

Women Who Write, Inc. is a 501(c)(3) organization. Donations are gratefully accepted to support the group's mission and are tax-deductible. The following books are publications of Women Who Write, and are available on www.Amazon.com and the Women Who Write website: www.womenwhowrite.com. They can also be purchased by mail.

Calliope: The 20th Annual Anthology (2013)
Calliope: The 19th Annual Anthology (2012)
Calliope: The 18th Annual Anthology (2011)
Calliope: The 17th Annual Anthology (2010)
Calliope: The 16th Annual Anthology (2009)
Home for the Holidays: Stories and Recipes (2011)
Comfort Cooking: Stories with Recipes (2010)

Order form on next page.

Order Form

Please send me _____ copies of *Calliope, the 20th Annual Anthology of Women Who Write* at $12 each, plus $3 each for shipping and handling. I have enclosed a check payable to Women Who Write for the total of $_____.

Mail order and check to:

Women Who Write
P.O. Box 6167
Louisville, KY 40206-0167

Ship books to:

Name _____

Address _____

City _____ State_____ Zip _____

Daytime phone (_____) _____-_____

Email address _____

Questions? Email us at info@womenwhowrite.com or director@womenwhowrite.com.

www.ingramcontent.com/pod-product-compliance
Lightning Source LLC
Chambersburg PA
CBHW072002170626
46813CB00005B/1974